D0855157

AMERICAN X

RA'UN SETI

ST. JOHN THE BAPTIST PARISH LIBRARY
2920 NEW HIGHWAY 51
LAPLACE, LOUISIANA 70068

AMERICAN X

Copyright © 2015 by ANUMENE PUBLICATIONS

All rights reserved. No part of this book may be reproduced or transmitted in any form or by any means without written permission from the author.

ISBN 978-1515100799

Table of Contents

Introduction

Like it or not, we Americans are people of habit. We tend to stay in uncomfortable situations that we've grown custom too, as long as they are tolerable. It's when the situation becomes intolerable that some of us begin marching in the streets for "change." Therefore, it is my moral duty as a so-called American to clearly explain the necessary truth in order that the unconscious masses of this nation might be set free from the illusion that they have been made to believe. Like for example, when they say; America is the land of the free; that individual Americans can own real property or that it's your right as an American citizen to walk down the street. These are the traditional perception we all have about this nation. But in all truth as Americans you don't have a full understanding of the way this country really operates or of their ultimate plan for a world government. In this book I will be going over topics which may have you scratching your head and asking the question about facts that are undeniable. I welcome both comments and criticism, so please feel free to contact me. I hope you will be enlightened by what you read. Our natural rights are lost through our own ignorance.

CHAPTER 1
LET'S GET RIGHT TO THE POINT

There are a lot of people out there that don't seem to be using what should come naturally to them and that is common sense. Do you remember what your teacher taught you about America in school? And how the American government was organized by the so – called founding fathers to ensure freedom and equality for the people of this land, and that the judiciary is designed to allow for fairness in resolving discrepancies between its citizens. How about when you got out in the real world and realized that your local city and state governments seemed to operate as if you was an illegal immigrate. Did that not make you wonder about what they taught you in class, that what they said was a big fat lie? And that the real world was just a big military camp? Do it not make you just want to pack up your stuff and leave the entire country or did you figured maybe that the various governments in this nation is always right no matter what they say or do because they are more qualified to make decisions for you.

Well, we all make mistakes. Believe me I've had my share of making the wrong choices in life, and paid for them. But there are some who will make the same wrong choices and be forgiven for them only because they have a little bit more money than you or that they are in a position of power.

For example I like to share with you an incident that happened to me that will give you a clear picture of what I'm saying. It was an early Monday morning and I was riding down highway 74 in Forest City North Carolina in an old black ford truck. I had stopped at a gas station to buy a bag of chips and a coke soda. After leaving the station I had turned on my favorite song, All Eyes on Me by 2-Pac Shakur. When some rookie looking cop pulls me over for a D.W.B which means Driving While Black. That was the only reason I could think of for why he would stopped me, but his excuse was that he pulled me over because I was driving on the yellow line. He then said that he was going to just give me a warning but he asked if I would step out of the car (what is this all about right!)

The next thing I know, I'm sitting in his passenger seat explaining to him that it is my constitutional right to refuse his search of my vehicle. He then informed me that a refusal is called for a search. He then had me to wait in his car while he searched

8

my vehicle for almost a half an hour. He then finally gave up when he found the unopened pack of potato chips and soda that I bought at the convenience store. So he let me go with a written warning.

Now will you like it if that happened to you?

Well, that's what I meant about those in power, they can do whatever they want and get away with it. Why? I tell you why, because the government is an idea, a fiction, and can only do business as a fiction, with a fiction. This is why they tried to shackle you with the fiction birth certificate, name and date of birth from the moment you open your eyes from your mother's womb. Now do you remember the movie Wizard of OZ? Well that movie wasn't just for entertainment; it was made shortly after the Federal Reserve Act, and it was Hollywood's way of showing Americans how to get their freedom back. Unfortunately, people didn't get it. For example, the first alter ego" who was with Dorothy walking with her along the yellow brick road was the straw man. If you look in any Black Law Dictionary you will find that it's a legal term. It means a fake person or dummy used as a bond. In Latin - a man of straw, one of no substance, put forward as a bail or surety.

Now how does this affect you? Look on your driver's license or your ID.... All capital letters. Look at the bottom of your license. Oh wow, you signed the contract! Do you reserve the right to be a human with the same name in that contract? Now under the rules recognized by modern courts, you must make a clear distinction between you, the facts, and this thing called the straw man, this is the only way you can expect your rights to be recognized in a modern day courtroom.

Now remember that in the movie Dorothy finds out that the Wizard was a complete fake an illusion just like the government, not a fact like yourself a living soul but a fiction.

Now let's dig in this subject a little deeper so that you can get a clearer picture of what I'm talking about. Now when a person is born in the United States they are given a Social Security Card, and with that comes income taxes. I am not going to go into how we have been put under (Admiralty) law; I will simply state that we are under it, but I will discuss this topic in another chapter.

Now let's talk about the license issue which is a privilege or permit to do things. A free American shouldn't have to require a license or permit. Why should a free American have to require permission from the government to get married, drive a car, or start a business, or to add on to his/her home or improve his/her property? Please show me in the U.S. Constitution or your state Constitution where a government has the right to demand such obedience? If anyone is arrogant enough to try to use the U.S. Constitution to show such a thing, don't bother because it's only going to make you look foolish. Now how did we get in such a mess, but more importantly how do we get out of such a mess?

Well it is said but don't take my word for it, I'm just the messenger. How to get out from under these provisions is to deny or denounce your US citizenship and receive diplomatic immunity. And for total freedom you also must file a UCC-1 lien against your straw man and a denial of corporate existence against the incorporated local and state governments.

Now have you ever noticed that your driver's license, bank statements, and any bills that you receive is in all capital letters? This is not by accident; there is a legal reason for this.

For example, did you ever wonder why the government or the state can take your house, property, cars, bank accounts, children etc.

Did you think that you owned everything you worked so hard for throughout your life?

Do you really thought you was truly free as nature intended it to be or are you a slave?

Are you a subject and paying dues to the crown of England through the tax system?

What is your real name? Is it John Doe, in all capital letters or is it John Doe in small case letters?

I know the answer, but do you?

So if you interested to know more I advise you to continue reading!

CHAPER 2
THE REASON YOU SHOULD NOT TRUST BANKS

Benjamin Franklin said in his biography that the inability of the colonists is to get the power to issue their own money permanently out of the hands of King George and the international bankers was the prime reason for the revolution war."

In 1913 was the third attempt by the European bankers to get their system back in place within the United States. It was when President Andrew Jackson was in office that the second effort was made in 1836. What they could not win militarily in the revolutionary war they attempt to accomplish by a banking money scheme which allow the European banks to own the mortgage on nearly every home, car, farm, ranch, and business at no cost to the bank. Making you the American people pay interest on the equity you lost, allowing the banks to take you for, hook, line and sinker.

Today people believe that cash and coins backs up writing checks. If you deposit a hundred dollars, the bank receives it as a bank asset and credits a demand deposit account, saying that the bank owes you a hundred dollars. For the hundred dollars your bank owes you, you may receive cash or write a check. If you write a one hundred dollar check, the hundred dollars your bank owes you is transferred to another bank and that bank owes one hundred dollars to the person you wrote the check to. That person can write a hundred dollar check or receive cash. So far there is no problem.

Remember one thing however, for the check to be valid there must first be a deposit of money to the bank's assets to make the check liable. See the liability is like a holding account claiming that the money was deposited to make the check good. Now all of this I just said should be common knowledge. But what is not so common is the fact that people don't have a clue about the unlawful practices of banks all over the nation and how the switch in currency takes place.

Now the bank advertises its loans and tells you to "sign here." But the bank never signs anything because they know they are not going to lend you their money or other depositor's money. Under the law of bankruptcy of a nation, the mortgage note becomes money. The bank makes it look like a loan but it is not. It is an exchange. When the bank receives the equity in the home you are buying for free, in exchange for an unpaid bank liability that the bank cannot pay without returning the mortgage note. If the bank had fulfilled its end of the contract, the bank could not have received the equity in your home for free.

Now when the bank receives your mortgage note without investing or risking one cent. The bank sells the mortgage note, receives cash or an asset that can then be converted to cash and still refuses to loan you money or other depositor's money or pay the liability it owes you. Now let's say you ask for a ten thousand dollar loan, the bank does not give up ten thousand. The bank receives ten thousand in cash or an asset and issues a ten thousand dollar liability check that the bank has no intention of paying. The ten thousand dollars that the bank receives in the alleged loan is the equity that the bank gets without investment, and it is the ten thousand dollars that the individual loses in equity to the bank, which the bank will demand him/her to pay plus interest.

Now back to that loan agreement the bank told you to sign. An agreement that the bank broke. The bank now owns the mortgage note without loaning anything. The bank then deposits the mortgage note in an account they open under your name without your authorization or knowledge. The bank then withdrawals the money without your authorization or knowledge using a bogus signature. So now the bank has claimed the money and the property, which is a fraudulent agreement.

15

HOW THE BANK SWITCHES THE CURRENCY

This is a repeat worded differently to be sure you understand where I'm going with this topic. Now you must understand that banks do not loan money. The bank just switches the currency. Now the alleged borrower creates the money by simply signing the mortgage note. The bank does not sign the mortgage note because they know they will not loan you their money. The mortgage note acts like money. To make it look like the bank loaned you money, the bank deposits your mortgage note as money from which to issue a check. There is no money loaned legally to fulfill a contract therefore the bank doesn't own the mortgage note. So by doing this, the bank received the lien on the property without risking or losing one cent. Then people loses the equity in their homes and land to the bank and now they must work to pay interest on the property, which the bank got for free.

It is very important to remember that a bank is not going to give you anything but a hard time. So whenever the bank says they gave you credit, they only meant they credited your transaction account, leaving you with the presumption that they deposited

16

other depositors money in the account. The truth is they deposited your money. The bank cannot claim they own the mortgage note until they loan you their money. If a bank deposits your money, they will credit a demand deposit account under your name so you can write checks and spend your money. So in reality they are claiming your money as theirs. Now ask a criminal attorney what happens in a fraudulent agreement of your funds to the banks use and benefit without you'll signature or authorization.

Now there has been several presidents like John Adams, Thomas Jefferson, and Abraham Lincoln. They all believed that banker capitalism was more dangerous to our liberties than standing armies. Pres. James Garfield said, "Whoever controls the money in any country is absolute master of industry and commerce.

Now I hope this explains exactly how the banks expand and contract the checkbook money supply forcing people into foreclosure. This could never happen if contracts were not violated and if we receive equal protection under the law of contract.

CHAPER 3

IS MONEY WHAT YOU THINK IT IS OR ANOTHER FORM OF CONTROL

There is nothing so admired, yet so misunderstood as money. All Americans spend most their lives laboring to acquire it. Many people measures a person's status in society by how much dough you hold. And nearly everything in our modern world is measured by its value.

But how many people in America have a clue what money is? Where it comes from? What gives it value? The history of it etc.? So what would you do if you knew what money really was?

Now pull out your dollar bill, look at it and ask yourself, where did this come from? What gives it value? Do you know what makes that green piece of paper money?

Now, before there was ever a thing as money, there was this thing called trade. Because back in the day people would trade one thing for another. This would only work if both traders wants what the other has. Otherwise, no deal. By having a commonly accepted third medium of exchange, expanded commerce became possible.

So coins, drilled shells, precious metals and animals were among the early forms of money. In the early forms of money, value came from the shortage of the material or the labor to produce it.

So how did that dead President in your hand become money? The answer was from this book I read years back called, *"The Creature from Jekyll Island"* this highly explosive and educational study on money covers the history of money, banking, wars and the political elite behind the money powers.

Now the story is that coins made of precious metals became the favorite medium of exchange in the olden days. The word money comes from the word, "Moneta," a nickname for the Roman goddess Juno. A temple to this goddess who was considered the guardian of the Roman treasury, was converted into a mint. The Romans began to call this temple "Moneta" and later used the name for other places where coins were made. So when the word Moneta evolved over the years to an abbreviated "mone" or Monet." The old English spelling of "monie" eventually became the word money

From primitive times through the last millennium there was a proliferation of coinage and various ways to degrade the coins by lightening their weight, coating it with less valuable metals. But the ultimate corruption came from the Goldsmiths in the 12th century who discovered the dirty scheme of fractional reserve holdings. The Goldsmiths issued paper receipts for gold they held in storage for their customers. The receipts came to be used as money since they could be returned to the Goldsmith for the gold held in storage.

The Goldsmiths knew that not everyone wanted their gold at once, so they issued more receipts than they had gold and got rich just with paper and ink. So this little strategy has been use by the elite ever since. This form of deception has been the root of the banking industry and will eventually put America in the worse financial crisis ever, do to greed.

WHAT IS MONEY

Money in the real sense of the word is gold coins or some other precious metal but not paper currency. Congress was only given the power in the Constitution to "coin money, regulate the value thereof, and of foreign coins." The Constitution does not authorize Congress to issue currency or create a central bank. So constitutionally only coins can be money.

The thing people need to understand is money is not something to be used "as" a medium of exchange, but that money "is" a medium of exchange, because money doesn't represent nothing, it's a note with no fundamental value.

Now my breakdown definition about money do not correlate the modern misguided notion of money. Now do you have gold coins in your bank account? When you write a check to someone, can they cash it for the face value in gold or silver coins? Or when you swipe your credit card or debit card at the gas pumps does a coin pop out of the card and into the pump to pay for your gas? I don't think so; so you don't really use money do you?

So in all reality we don't have money, what we use as money has become money to every citizen in America. As an advocate of constitutional reality, I always find myself debating with people on this issue who have lost all sense of reality. How can I explain the value of precious metal coin money that "is" a medium of exchange, to the members of the current masses who have been brainwashed into believing that the Federal Reserve notes, credit cards and bank accounts are money or that they have money in them?

THE FOUR DIFFERENT TYPES OF MONEY

Now the dollar that you have in your hand has been in the "fiat money" phase for almost 70 years, one of the longest running fiat schemes that the elite have yet developed. To understand the nature of the fiat scheme we must first discuss the three other forms of money and see how they all relate.

COMMODITY MONEY

Commodity money is just that. Gold, silver or copper coins; animal skins, liquor, sugar or salt. When the American colonies became productive they were short on money but loaded with tobacco. Bundles of tobacco where widely accepted in colonial docks as commodity money to purchase the goods imported from

Europe. On the return trip, merchants accepted tobacco as money for more goods purchased for shipment to the New World.

Just like gold, which has been preferred as commodity money for thousands of years. It is very rare, it doesn't spoil or decay, and unlike jewels, it is extremely valuable. It also creates stability in a free market society. The supply of the commodity money will naturally regulate its value relative to the products and services available in a given society. So the myth that there isn't enough gold to go around is just nonsense, that the amount of gold available and the items available in commerce would not change, only the measurement we use between them.

RECEIPT MONEY

Now receipt money is plainly a receipt for commodity money. It is used "as" money. If it remains one hundred percent back by the commodity it does no harm. It's manageable and can be very valuable if, for example, the receipt entitles the holder to a large stack of precious coins.

Normally, receipt money offers some terms of redemption such as "payable to bearer on demand."

The only problem with receipt money is when by some fraud, legal or otherwise, is turned into fractional money. The Goldsmiths founded that concept which was one of the steps along the way to make that almighty dollar in your hand today.

FRACTIONAL MONEY

Fractional money is what happens when more receipt money is circulated than there is commodity money to redeem it with. Only a fraction of the substance is there to back the promise to pay. Fractional money is the direct result of people's greed, meaning the desire to get something for nothing.

Now do you want to know why there has been so many government shutdowns in the past two decades or so? It's because the government has been getting caught with their pants down. Understand this, if commodity money demanded doesn't match the fractional money in circulation, there are three things that could happen. A total collapse of the economic system involved; a partial collapse of the financial unit where it is devalued to match the commodity money; or a conversion to fiat money.

FIAT MONEY

Fiat money is often defined as paper currency not backed by gold or silver. It is sometimes enforced by "legal tender" laws which force people to accept it even though it has no real value. "Fiat" is a Latin word for "let it be done," as in a random order or decision.

Fiat money is what we have "let it be done" to our economy, which constitutionally is required to be a commodity money system of coins. There are reasons why the American founders mandated a coin based economy.

When the fiat paper hit the scene in the 1690s. Massachusetts was the first to use it as a means to finance its military raids against the French colony in Quebec. The other colonies were quick to follow suit and within a couple of years they were in a custom of printing 'paper of I owe you notes." As one colonial legislator said at that time.

"Do you think gentlemen that I will consent to load my constituents with taxes when we can send to our printer and get a whole wagon load of money, one quire of which will pay for the whole?"

Now there is a hidden tax called inflation associated with the issuance of fiat money. Because inflation is the natural result whenever more currency is added to a given economy. The value of the existing currency is deflated relative to the amount of new currency issued and circulated. By the late 1750s Connecticut had price inflated by eight hundred percent, the Carolinas had inflated nine hundred percent. Fiat inflation was so out of hand that the British stepped in and banned the production of fiat money.

But what happened next was unforeseen by the marketers of fiat money. Among great sadness about insufficient money, a marvel fortune happened. The force use to make fiat money had compelled everyone to store their real money and use the worthless paper cash instead. Now that the paper was a shame, the colonists began to use their English, French and Dutch gold coins again, prices rapidly adjusted to reality, and commerce returned to a solid footing. It remained so even during the economic strain of the war of 1756 and during the period immediately prior to the Revolution War. Here was a perfect example of how an economic system in distress can recover if the government does not interfere with the healing process.

This is not the end of fiat currency in the colonies. Due to the cost of the war, it had initiate the printing process again.

At the beginning of the war in 1775, the total financial supply for the federated colonies stood at 12 million. In June of that year, the Continental Congress issued another 2 million. And before the notes were printed, another 1 million was approved. And on top of this the states were doing the same in a roughly equal amount.

And still more, when the Continental Army was unable to get enough money from Congress, they issued certificates for the purchase of supplies totaling over 200 million. The result? In 1775, colonial money called the Continental was worth one dollar in gold. In 1778 it was valued at 25%. By 1779 it was worth less than a penny.

Thomas Jefferson clearly explain the nature of the hidden tax called inflation:

"It will be asked how the two masses of Continental and of state money have cost the people of the United States $27 million, when they are to be redeemed now with about 6 million? I answer that the difference being 66 million has been lost on the bills separately by the successive holders of them. Everyone, through

whose hands a bill passed, lost on that bill what it lost in value during the time it was in his hands. This was a real tax on him, and in this way the people of the United States actually contributed those millions of dollars during the war, and by a mode of taxation the most oppressive of all."

Is there any questions in your mind now as to why in the beginning that the power holders of this nation only gave Congress the power to coin money. It was once said that this is a favorable moment to shut and bar the door against paper money. This mischief of the various experiments which have been made are now fresh in the public mind and have excited the disgust of all the respectable parts of America.

Not all fiat money follows a progression from commodity money, to receipt money, to fractional money, to fiat money. Many other colonial currencies began and ended as fiat money. The modern "Euro" is nothing more than pure fiat money.

THE FRACTIONAL FIAT

What is "fractional?" Money that has been invented by the elite. It's not really a separate form of money in our working definition of money, but it could be called fractional fiat money. Instead of fractional money where only a fraction of the commodity money is kept on hand, a fractional portion of the fiat money is used by the financial institution as a basis to make loans. It is more commonly referred to as fractional reserves. The reserves are kept on hand just like the Goldsmith's fractional gold to pay out to the suspecting customers and keep them unsuspecting.

The fractional reserve rate is carefully calculated by the financial elite at the Fed to keep our fiat world rolling a head. Fractional fiat money is part of the grand scheme to create money out of nowhere. I will go over this again later but right now I would like to break down the illusion of that green paperback you call a dollar in your hand.

THE LONG HISTORY OF ECONOMIC TREACHERY

So how did that dollar bill in your hand become money? The first thing to understand is that the Federal Reserve Bank is not part of the federal government. Most of you Americans fail to realize this fact.

The real purpose of the Federal Reserve is to stop the growing competition from the nation's newer banks and by doing so is to build a franchise to create money out of nothing for the purpose of lending, and getting control of the reserves of all banks so that the more reckless ones would not be exposed to currency drains and bank runs, get the taxpayers to pick up the cartel's unavoidable losses, and tell Congress that the reason was to protect the public.

It was in 1910 that the Federal Reserve Bank became the fourth and current experiment in the United States central banking. The history of that experiment, and the wars, chaos, and turmoil caused by it are already the subject of many books. I can't begin to break down its history in this book so I will just write a small portion of what I know of the Fed's transition through the four forms of money and how the Fed's deliberately manipulated the world.

In 1913, the Fed was created by the Federal Reserve Act. Congress also gave away many of its treasury buildings to the Fed and the Fed's seized control of the nation's gold stores. In the true nature of the European bankers who is controlling everything behind the scenes, the Fed began bamboozling America.

The Federal Reserve notes which apparently began as receipt money, "payable to holder on demand," was soon converted to fractional money. But many more Federal Reserve notes were issued than they had gold to back them. It was said that the Fed had made loans of gold – backed "dollars" to its member banks in an amount that was six times the world's known gold supply, and that much of American's gold supply was being shipped overseas in trade for German currency and other paper assets.

Heavily fractionalized, the booming 20s was fueled by infusions of Fed fractional money. This continued until the Fed tightened the purse strains, contracting the money supply and causing the crash of 1929 which brought about the Great Depression. By the spring of 1933, a lot of Americans figured out there wasn't enough gold in the vaults to "pay to bearer on demand," so they made a run on the banks to get their gold while they could.

To prevent a collapse of the Fed, Pres. Roosevelt declared a banking holiday and close the banks by Executive Order. Congress soon follow suit and declared that Fed notes were no longer redeemable in gold. Fed fractional money became Federal fiat money with the acts of a complaint and complicit President and Congress. Why would elected politicians who only want to get re-elected violate the trust of the people and the laws of the Constitution, in favor of a private central bank?

THE CONCLUSION

Now it's easy to say fiat money is made out of paper and ink, but there is more to it than that. If it were that easy, more people besides the Montana Freeman would be doing it. The magic of flat money is something bankers, presidents and congressmen would do anything for.

Griffin, in The Creature from Jekyll Island, says this magic that he called the "Mandrake Mechanism" after the 1940s comics strip character "Mandrake the Magician." Mandrake specialty was making things out of nothing and making them disappear back into the same void. "In truth, money is not created until the instant it is borrowed, It is the act of borrowed that causes it to spring into existence. And incidentally, it is the act of paying off the debt that causes it to vanish... In spite of the technical nonsense and seemingly complicated procedures, the actual tool by which the Federal Reserve makes money is quite easy. They do it exactly the same way the Goldsmiths did it, except of course the Goldsmiths were limited by the need to hold some precious metal and reserve, whereas the Fed has no such restriction.

It is difficult for Americans to come to grips with the fact that their total money supply is backed by nothing but debt, and it is even more mind-boggling to visualize that if everyone paid back all that was borrowed, there would be no money left in existence."

To prove what I'm saying, back in 1941 Gov. Mariner Eccles testified before the House Committee on banking and Currency, he was asked how the Fed got the money to purchase two billion dollars' worth of government bonds in 1933. Eccles replied and said. *"We created it."* And he was then asked. *"Out of what?"* He replied. *"Out of the right to issue credit money."* The next question was asked. *"And there is nothing behind it, is there?"*

"Except our government's credit?" Eccles responded. *"That is what our money system is. If there were no debts in our money system there wouldn't be any money."*

What Americans must understand is that when banks placed credits into your account, they are simply pretending to lend you money. In truth, they have nothing to lend. Even the money that non - indebted depositors have placed with them was originally created out of nothing in response to someone else's loan. So what allows the banks to collect rent on nothing? It is irrelevant for us Americans to be forced to accept these worthless certificates in exchange for real goods and services.

So the bottom line is this here. Congress and the banking cartel have entered into a partnership in which the cartel has the privilege of collecting interest on money which is made out of nothing, a perpetual override on every American dollar that exist in the world. Congress, on the other hand has access to unlimited funding without having to tell the American people that their taxes are being raised through the process of inflation.

So how does all this happen? First, the government puts ink on a piece of paper called a Treasury Bond or what I like to call I owe you notes, which is a promise to pay a certain sum with interest at a certain date. The note is then given to the Fed where it is classified as a securities "asset." It is called an asset because it is assumed that the government will pay it back with money from future taxation. This "asset" can be used to offset a liability, so the Fed creates a liability by putting ink on another piece of paper called a Federal Reserve check, which it exchanges with the government in exchange for the "asset."

But the problem with this situation is that there is no money in any account to cover this check. If it was one of us doing this we would be in prison. It is legal for the Fed however, because Congress wants the money, and this is the easiest way to get it. This way the process is mysteriously wrapped up in the banking system. The end result however, is the same as turning on the government printing presses and simply manufacturing fiat money to pay government expenses. Yet, in accounting terms, the books are said to be balanced because the liability of the check is offset by the asset of the bond.

The Fed check is then endorsed and deposited in a Federal Reserve Bank where it becomes a government deposit. It can then be used to pay the government expenses by issuing government checks. This begins the first flood of the manufacture of fiat money. The government checks are either deposited or cashed, adding to the M-1 money supply as an account balance or circulating currency. The deposit government checks become commercial bank deposits,

Now what you have to understand is that commercial bank deposits can immediately take on a split personality. On the one hand, they are liabilities to the bank because they are owed back to the depositors. But as long as they remain in the bank, they are considered as assets because they are on hand. Once again, the books are balanced, the assets offset the liabilities. But the process does not stop there. Through the fractional reserve banking, the deposits are made to serve an additional and more profitable purpose. To accomplish this, the on hand deposits now become reclassified in the books and called bank reserves.

"Reserves for what? Are these for paying off depositors should they want to close out their accounts? No." That's the

common function they served when they were classified as plain assets. Now that they have been given the name of 'reserves,' they become the magic stick to materialize even larger amounts of fiat money. This is where the real action is, at the level of the commercial banks.

Now here's how it works. The banks are permitted by the Fed to hold as little as 10% of their deposits and reserves. That means if they receive deposits of $1 million from the first wave of fiat money made by the Fed, they have $900,000 more than they are required to keep on hand. In bankers' language, that $900,000 is called excess reserves. Now that they have been transmuting into an excess, they are considered available for lending. And so in due course these excess reserves are converted into bank loans.

"But how can this money be loaned out when it is owned by the original depositors who are still free to write checks and spend it anytime they wish? Isn't that a double claim against the same money? The answer is that when the new loans are made, they are not made with the same money at all. They are made with brand new money created out of thin air for that purpose. The nation's money supply simply increases by 90% of the bank's deposits.

Also, this new money is far more interesting to the banks than the old. The old money which they received from the depositors requires them to pay out interest or perform services for the privilege of using it. But with the new money, the banks collect interest instead, which is not too bad considering it cost them nothing to make.

So when this second flood of fiat money goes into our economy, it comes right back into the banking system just as the first wave did, in the form of more commercial bank deposits. The process now repeats itself but with slightly smaller numbers each time around. The deposit is then reclassified as a reserve and 90% of that becomes an 'excess reserve' which, once again is available for a new loan. Therefore, the 1 million of the first wave of fiat money give birth to 900,000 in the second wave, and that gives birth to 810,000 in the third wave ($900,000 less 10% reserve). It takes about 28 times through the revolving door of deposits to become loans, becoming deposits, becoming more loans, until the process plays itself out to the maximum effect which is [that] the amount of fiat money created by the banking cartel is approximately nine times the amount of the original government debt which made the entire process possible.

So when the original debt itself is added to that figure, we finally have roughly ten times the amount of the underlying government debt. To the degree that this newly created money floods into the economy in excess of goods and services, it causes the purchasing power of all money, both old and new to decline. Prices go up because the relative value of the money has gone down. The result is the same as if that purchasing power had been taken from us in taxes. The reality of this process therefore is that it is a hidden tax up to ten times the national debt.

Without realizing it, Americans have paid in addition to the regular taxes, a complete hidden tax equal to many times the national debt! And that is still not the end of the process. Since our money supply is purely arbitrary with nothing behind it except debt, its number can go down as well as up. When people are going deeper into debt, the nation's money supply expands and prices go up, but when they pay off their debts and refused to renew, the money supply contracts and prices tumble. This change between periods of expansion and contradiction of the money supply is the underlying cause of booms, busts and depressions.

The only beneficiaries are the political elite in Congress, who enjoy the effect of unlimited revenue to maintain their power, and the financial elite within the cartel called the Federal Reserve System who have been able to bind the American people without them knowing it.

Now do you understand how Congress, the US Treasury, and the Federal Reserve have been operating? Do you see why Pres. Roosevelt and Congress ignored the obvious, and took the people's gold to protect the bankers scheme in 1933?

In history, most fiat money schemes goes on for only a few years. The Fed has been running their scheme in total fiat mode for almost 70 years. The elite have mastered their fraud to a fine art, keeping tight control and making adjustments to extract their rule over every last drop of American productivity without creating the collapse of their otherwise dull scheme. Their partners at the International Monetary Fund and the World Bank, also makers of the U.S. Congress have stretched the fiat money gross around the planet.

So now you know where that "dollar" bill in your hand came from. Does it still look like the dollar bill you thought it was when you started reading this chapter?

CHAPTER 4

THE FEDERAL RESERVE IS NOT WHAT IT APPEARS TO BE

The Federal Reserve is a privately owned banking system, which allows banks to legally counterfeit eight times the amount of money they hold in deposits. A system of exponential inflation and debt. A system designed to flop. The usurpation and silent cup of this government has occurred.

The Federal Reserve act became the most gigantic trust on earth. When Pres. Wilson put in this bill, the invisible government of the monetary power became legalized... The worst legislative crime of the ages is committed by this banking and currency bill.

This is where inflation comes from. The legal counterfeiting by banks through loans. When you get a loan, the bank doesn't give you money from their deposit holdings, they make it up out of thin air and keep their money. This added imaginary money to the economy, lowers the value of the existing money, and with every loan causes inflation. If you don't pay back the counterfeit loan, they take your very real house, with guns, and still have the same amount of money in their deposits that they started with before the loan, plus any payment money you previously made. And don't forget about the imaginary interests. A bank makes a profit and gets your assets to resell again for even more profit if you default on that loan or credit card. And they do it at gunpoint. It's the greatest rip-off of all time along with the Federal Income tax, which is also enforced by a gun. A bank only loses money if people withdrawal from it or close their accounts with the bank, not if you default on a loan.

Contrary to popular belief, the Federal Reserve is not regulated by the government at all, but by mostly offshore private, unelected bankers. These private banks loans money to the government with interest, and all of it is an illusion. Nearly every

President from Obama on down since the Federal Reserve was created has been a puppet to these private bankers, except Kennedy. And we all know what happened to him.

THE ABOLITISHMENT OF THE GOLD STANDARD

The dollar became the world's first reserve currency on the planet because it was the only non-fiat currency in the world that was backed up by gold. It is how America became so great, because its money was as good as gold. This standard was removed by the treasonous Nixon in 1971, and was the major promoter to the current economic crisis which truly made the financial system completely unreal, and controlled by the very few. History shows that all fiat currencies are unsustainable and always fails, yet they allow it to happen. Once the gold standard was removed, the fiat dollar was destined and designed to flop.

Because the dollar is the world's reserve currency, the crisis goes global as we see it today. This action allowed the banks to invent as much money as they wanted out of nothing, and that's how things like the hugely expensive Cold War and the so-called war on terror was created and funded on both sides with interests.

putting the people in massive debt. These same offshore bankers who run the Federal Reserve, also runs most other countries central banks too. And these bankers have funded both sides of every conflict for a very, very long time. Such like the oil companies supply oil to both sides and Wall Street investing money to both sides. They work together and played countries off each other while they reap profits and either kill, or put the population in debt, and steal their freedoms. This is how the military industrial complex, the medical industrial complex, and the corporate industrial complex, Wall Street, and government itself has become the most calculating devils they are today. They all work together against everyone.

This was also the main reason they started off-shoring most of everyone's jobs. The US currency was no longer as good as gold and it was now more profitable for corporations to ship their businesses overseas to places like India and China. This was the beginning of the major devaluation of the dollar and the beginning of the job crisis. People saw the beginning of the rise of India and China at that moment since they were now getting all the good jobs. But they are also in great danger too, because now they hold most of all the world's reserves like the dollar which is now weakening, all because of these bankers.

THE FAKE WAR ON TERROR:

9/11 was a plan to change American foreign and domestic policies to pre-emptive war, even nuclear, and began the even more massive increase of government and government spending on defense, which in turn is causing huge inflation and huge debt for everyone. War accelerates the destruction of currency and increases debt and that is why the economic crisis has grew since the war on terror began. The so-called freedom here in America has been removed with the Patriot-Act, which is nearly the same thing that Hitler did with his Enabling Act, which he instituted on his people to legally round up the political rebellious lawyers, journalists, labor unions, professors, students, artists, and of course the so-called Jews which I like to call Khazars who don't have any historical or genetic connections to the ancient Hebrews only that they stole the culture and ran with it. But that's another subject, now back to what I was saying. This was immediately after he burned down his own German Parliament building, the

45

Reichstag. He blamed it on communist terrorists and adopted pre-emptive war. After 9/11 the government adopted pre-emptive war, created a national homeland security just as Hitler did, and in 2009 new legislation was introduced to authorize and activate concentration camps here in America just as Hitler did. This bill is called H.R. 645. Check it out for yourself. America will now spend more money on defense every year than the rest of the world does combined. A collapsed is guaranteed. This is Nazi Germany all over again in slow motion.

CHAPTER 5

HOLOCAUST OR HOLOHOAX

I know that this subject is going to be a little sensitive to some people who may get their hands on this book and come across this chapter, but I had to throw this topic out there. Because when someone tells me something I just don't take it for face value, I go out and do my research. Now whenever the subject about the Holocaust is mentioned they talk about it as if it was the greatest tragedy that had ever happen in human history, but what gets me is that there was twice as many mongoloid natives that died here in America than World War I and 2 combined, and not to mention that there were more Africans that died during the slave trade than all the American wars put together. But you don't see them talking about that in school, why? Because it's the truth, they don't won't the truth interfering with their agenda, if so then everything that they have accomplished will come tumbling down. Why do you think they like telling you the story that Christopher Columbus discovered America when everyone knows that's a lie, what they should say is 'when Christopher Columbus was discovered.'

I couldn't never understand why they would want to push a whole nation of people out of the picture. So when they realize that wasn't going to fly they sidetracked their story and said, 'oh no, we meant to say that he was the first European to discovered America, but that was also a lie too. It was the Vikings who was the first Europeans to come to America. So after that they this just gave up and said, 'yeah you right it was the Native Americans, but again they were wrong.

Now I had always believe that Native Americans or Mongoloid Americans which I like to call them were the first people in America, but after years of research I found out that these people that came across the Bering Straits out of Asia sum 3000 years ago were not the first Americans. I found out that the oldest bones ever discovered in America belong to people from Africa, called Pygmies dating back over 56,000 years ago, but that's another story. I just wanted to make a point that just because it's in his-story book doesn't mean it's true. Now back to the subject at hand, Okay for example if the state of Texas is seven times the size of Germany with only 26 million people with everything else in between, and Germany holding 80 million people with anything between. So how does this all add up, actually it doesn't. What I figure is that they want you to believe that Germany has this large population in order to make it sound possible that 6 million so-called Jews could had died in the Holocaust, just saying.

Because this alleged story of millions of so-called Jews being tortured in concentration camps, has been proven time and time again to be inaccurate, for the acclaimed number of murder Jews to be true is impossible, proven not only by logic, but also the fact that the survivors of these events have been known to and even admitted to being paid to lie about it. This in itself should be proof enough of this act of misleading propaganda being false, but there is indeed more evidence. One reason to believe that the Holocaust is a lie is that the so-called Jews claim to have been murder in gas chambers, one group at a time. However, no evidence of such occurrences has been shown or documented. According to the medical scientists who were assigned to study the bodies of the victims, said that some of them died from typhus epidemics. And most of them died from starvation and lack of medical care resulting from allied bombing raids against food and medical supply lines.

They showed pictures of completely clothed women and children, claiming that they were force into cage camps and were stripped of their belongings and brutally killed. But again, the truth lies in the fact that the Germans were against typhus, which was the real reason for shaving heads, fumigating buildings, and cremating corpses.

Also, heads were shaved and people were gathered to be treated not with lethal gases in order to commit genocide, but with repellant, to stop the epidemic of lice spreading throughout the camps. Another thing that contradicts their story is that the number of so-called Jews killed in the camps was inaccurate, stating that 6 million so-called Jews were supposedly killed in the Holocaust, when not even such an amount existed in Europe entirely, let alone Germany. In 1939 there were nearly over 15 million proclaimed Jews in the world. After the Second World War that number had risen to over 18 million proclaimed Jews. What this means is that of the 15 million proclaimed Jews on the planet, 6 million were gassed, leaving only some 9,000,000+, in the world. Then the Jewish population rebounded and double to over 18 million in less than nine years, and amazing feat which astonished the minds of biologists and baby doctors everywhere! Not only were the so-called Jews not murder, but were given a choice of staying to be liberated by the communist or go with their Germany captors, they did not hesitate to choose the first option! Thus proving that the Jewish population was not forced to concentration camps to be scalped and gassed. Not only is there proof that the Holocaust is a lie, but also some very trustworthy witnesses like the American Red Cross who was asked to do an investigation on the camps and corpse, stated that in the chaotic condition of Germany after the invasion during the final months of the war, the camps received no food supplies at all and starvation claimed an increasing number of victims. In reading this, one may conclude that the Germans did not intensively kill the so-called Jews, but attempted to maintain lives.

Many of the allegations against the Germans involving gas chambers, which the so-called Jews claim that they were stripped, shaved, and gather to be slaughtered like cattle. However, in order for a gas chamber to exist there must be airtight doors in high chimneys, neither of which was found at the death camps. Also there is no proof of one single gassed so-called Jew, except for allegations made by hired phony witnesses. According to the Red Cross, not one single body has ever been autopsied and found to have died of gas poisoning. I have seen pictures of dead bodies on TV from World War ll, but most of these deaths I have learned occurred from starvation or bombings, and a great many of those were murdered Germans, there should be 12 football fields packed full of gassed bodies to present as evidence, yet not one body has ever been discovered.

If this is not proof enough then what else is there to say? What excuse can be made in reply? This is not to say that the Holocaust did not take place. I'm just trying to prove that it did not happen as it was told according to these conspires, it is just like when they said that Saddam Hussein had weapons of mass destruction and there were none to be found. You got to understand these people will lie in order to fulfill a certain agenda or goal, the invasion of Iraq was for its oil, and nothing more. And the illusion of a massive Holocaust was created to justify an illegal occupation of Palestine. Finally, without being given the evidence that it did happen as it is told, you are shown clues that the effects on Europe due to World War II was much different; not a story that would benefit the so-called Jews, given the fact that they are compensated each month for something that was simply a Holohoax.

CHAPTER 6

THE GOVERNMENT IS USING MASS MEDIA, TO MANIPULATE THE WAY YOU THINK, AND PERCEIVE THE WORLD

I can show in detail the many ways in which you and everyone you know are being brutally molested by TV, movies, and the media. This molestation is not sexual; so don't take my words out of context, it's mental, emotional, and above all, totally psychologically. For example, religion organizations will profit off the misery of others. For the past four decades, America has been bombarded with millions of heart wrenching images on television of poor people starving to death in Africa, and in some South American countries. We would think that these organizations have already gone through so many campaigns to get massive foodstuff and supplies to these areas, which now is starting to get old. People are starting to get fed up with it all, and are undoubtedly starting to ask questions. So where is all them millions of dollars that has been donated to those people go too? Well I tell you, in the hands, and pockets of those religion organizations who are behind the propaganda. They will say that this child or that person needs your help, now they have went as far as to say that this poor dog or cat needs saving, and you know there's plenty of people in America that loves animals. These organizations are taking advantage of your sympathy and using it to gain financially.

MEDIA MANIPULATION

Media ownership is central to the manipulation of the people. You either control the media by owning it or by doing favors for those who own it. In America, large corporations own the media and these in turn receive favors from the government in the form of influence over legislations and special tax breaks. There are only about five major-media corporations that controls almost all of the US media, which is why the American people are among the most ignorant and brainwashed people in the world.

TELEVISION OR TELL-LIE-VISION

Television has done more harm to society than any other medium. It has shortened attention spans with its six seconds soundbites, presenting us with a diet of dissociated facts and insignificances, completely out of any historical or sociological context, usually with an emotional charge to keep you watching. In its fairground approach, serious questions and reasoning is replaced by slick emotional fantasy, discussions is reduced to a screaming match between two opposing extremists in a foolishly divided debate, and the reality of even serious matters such as rape and murder is reduced to entertainment. It would not be an overstatement to say that television, in its present form, is the rival of true democracy. Although no one see's it, here are several examples how tell-lie-vision works its magic to make you see things their way.

EVERLASTING WARS

A country at war with an enemy in or out is usually a country that is united in fear, and one in which the people are happy to hand over power to their leaders. The ideal of being at war, and in danger makes the handing over of all power to a small rulering class seems to be the unavoidable condition for survival. Until a decade ago, Iraq, and their supporting allies represented this danger for the United States. Upon its collapsed however, there was a rise in civil liberties until the US was able to start a new war to disguise its imperialist and tyrannical ambitions: *THE WAR ON TERROR*. Since the talk of this terror crap, a huge amount of freedoms have been taken away from the people under the umbrella of national security. The war on terror has the added advantage of being unbeatable and therefore continually serves those who wants power. It's a saying that, people can always be brought to the bidding of their leaders by telling them they are being attacked, and denounce the peacemakers for lack of patriotism and exposing the country to danger. This can also work in other countries as well.

THE GIFT OF GAB

The language that the media use definitely manipulates the reality and the behavior of people. As they say war is peace; a doublespeak threateningly mirrored by Bush during a speech about the war in Iraqi when he made the statement saying that, 'the war in Iraq is really about peace." The attack on Iraq was continually referred to as liberation and the US military called it "Operation Iraq Freedom' of course liberation and freedom had little to do with the real reason that the US and the UK invaded that country, but the rhetoric at least allows concerned citizens an excuse to deceive themselves into supporting deliberate colonization. Other terms that was used by the military was collateral damage' for civilian casualties and the axle of evil, which gives the impression that countries with different ideologies to that of the US are somehow plotting together to hurt the US, when in fact most of these countries have almost no diplomatic relationships with each other. Don't you see that the whole aim of World News, Fox, CNN is to narrow the range of thought? In the end, every news network should be hold countable for manipulation, and perjury.

BLIND PATRIOTISM

At first patriotism might seem a show of unity and pride for your country, but it is actually one of the main methods that people are manipulated into serving their government in ways that may not be in their best interest. Because as long as people are patriotic, they will overlook the wrongs of their government, both towards their own people, and towards those in other countries. When back in 2004 Prime Minister Blair was asked if he had any regrets over Iraq, he avoids the question and turns the focus to patriotism saying, "*I think our boys have done a fantastic job*," basically implying that anyone who questions the legitimacy of the Iraq invasion questions the legitimacy of our boys. This tendency for strong arm robbery to ride on a movement of patriotism is particularly running rampant in America.

A POLLUTED EDUCATION SYSTEM

It is stupid to believe that only the uneducated can be manipulated. I think that the most educated ones are actually the easiest to brainwash because they have been programmed to process so much information that they often become less critical. The educated ones also tend to need an opinion on everything. The school system today is designed to manufacture individuals to support government propaganda. When back in the day school kids were more revolutionary and would question the actions of society, today it would seem that the revolutionary spirit has died due to the influence of 'Big Brother, and their corporations.

MODERN DAY SLAVERY

Corporations are like slave plantations that force people to work long hours for little of the overall profits. When people work for these corporations they are used to overbearing environments and are left with little time to concern themselves with the things that goes on in society and the world. This makes people very vulnerable to government manipulation because they are so used to being manipulated at work, and being a slave to a system. I think that the attitude of working long and intense hours, something that even slaves back in the day were not exposed too, is a good thing for society as it raises anybody's standard of living. This may be true to some extent, but it is still an underhanded operation, and in a so-called democracy you would think people should be a least conscious of this fact.

FEAR IS ALSO USED AS A FORM OF CONTROL

Fear is one of the best ways to control people... fear of riots, bigotry, war, and discrimination, and the list goes on. Fear is used to manipulate people into receiving life-threatening and expensive medical treatments, weapons, and home security systems. They even got you giving money to cancer charities, most of which is waste on chemotherapy that can have you worse off than no treatment at all. They got you going to church so that you won't go to hell, and being a corporate slave so that you don't find yourself throw out on the streets by your mortgage company. In fact, fear is the best weapon for the government, corporations, and religious organizations.

NEVER ADMIT A LIE

A friend had always told me just simply keep repeating it. This works well for the government, who continues to mislead its citizens. This is why 85% of the American people still believe that Saddam and Bin Laden were behind 9/11 despite all evidence to the contrary. The media propaganda machine just keep repeating it over and over. That weapons of mass destruction did exist and that it was a good thing to illegally invade a sovereign nation.

ADVERTISEMENT CONTROL

When you live in an environment flooded with corporate advertising, you grow used to their presence. You also expect to be manipulated into buying something or other. The way that most advertising is conducted is to hook you on an emotional response rather than engaging our cerebral cortex, the idea being that more primitive responses of the brain are more predictable and so the outcome of the advertising is more certain. What we don't realize is that these techniques are being used to sell you more than just products or services. They are being used by the government and corporations to sell you ideals and worldviews that support the government and the corporations. There are billions of dollars being spent in the buildup of wars around the world by the government, and they are manipulating the American people into supporting their madness.

MASSIVE DEBT

A people and a nation in debt is far easier to manipulate than one that isn't because its members are so busy trying to pay off their mortgages and pay their bills. A lot of people don't have time or the energy to challenge the status quo. The average person is deliberately kept just short from becoming broke or homeless, so he remains a slave to the system. Debt also applies to nations where it is used brutally by the developed countries to enslave undeveloped countries and steal their resources.

THE ENTERTAINMENT HYPNOSIS

Almost everyone is glued to their television for hours a day, and many of them spends a huge amount of time playing video games, and on the Internet. Movie stars and musicians are now our main role models, with a level of influence that only very few real icons could ever match. Entertainment has become toxic, clouding the minds from challenging anything of importance, and giving those who are manipulate you a far easier task. The main way to keep rating high on national television is to appeal to the primitive emotions of the four devils, fled, feed, fight, and fornicate. This sensationalism is one of the main reasons for the negative effect on society, and its alarming distortion of reality.

GOVERNMENT INTIMIDATION

Now of course, if everything above don't work, then those in power can resort to physical intimidation. I had a friend who was locked up with me that was beaten by four correctional officers for just refusing to not get his dreadlocks cut off, saying that he was a Rastafarian, and that it was his religious right to keep them. In the United Police State of American, intimidation is used to keep people in line, and it is absolutely incorrect to believe that physical abuse of captives only happens in other countries. The United States illegally holds and tortures their enemies in Guantanamo Bay every day which is a complete violation of the Geneva Convention. This is an amazing example by the so-called leaders of democracy to say to the world and to the American people is that might is right, and so is torture.

All these methods and situations above are used to manipulate society. Of course, it has been argued that some manipulation is necessary in order to have people to fulfill their functions or roles in society. For example, the goal is to become part of corporate America. (1). have a couple of kids. (2). submissively pay off your mortgage, and like a dumb ass go off to war like a pig to the slaughterhouse to defend a country that don't care nothing about you. Otherwise, the forces forbid the corporate world will fall, people might have no children or have 10 out of wedlock, the banks might lose the interest that they charge on imaginary currency, and a lot of innocent women and children might be murdered in far off countries or by state sponsored medical poisons. What some call the positive or vital role of this manipulation or propaganda still takes away power from the people and puts it into a social structure that benefits the few at the expense of the many. This clearly violates the ideals of a true democracy in which the people hold the power and make the decisions.

Because history do bear testimony to the disasters and suffering that happens when the people do not hold the power. They must reduce the level of manipulation so that they can begin to act consciously in their own interests rather than unconsciously in the interest of the few, such as politicians, big business, the military, banks, and so on.

CHAPTER 7

ORGAN HARVESTING

Yes that's right, to some the only conceivable way to live indefinitely is to have an organ transplant. The medical facilities are operating with huge grants from the government and private sources, pouring in untold millions of dollars into organ transplant research. Their success has been phenomenal, as many Americans are alive today because of this newly developed skill.

But success has its price tag. This procedure has become so popular, and so widely used, that in today's society there is a lot more demand for human organs for transplant than there are organs available. This situation has led to higher prices for organs, which in some cases seem almost impossible to get.

The elite are working in great secrecy with their doctors in many hospitals around the nation, and are literally declaring their patients brain dead or some other type of reason on why that person is deceased, and literally stealing his or her organs. Of course the patient is now really dead, and their body is removed. Later a fake death certificate is issued listing the cause of death that sounds believable. This is very similar to what happened in Nazi Germany in the mid-1930s. Once the state became involved in the death making in Germany, doctors boldly killed people whom they declared that their lives were worthless. After the victim had been killed, they would issue a fake death certificate.

Of course the one factor present in America today is that this same copycat mentality is joined with American greed, as there is much money to be made in the harvesting of organs. There is already something of a black market for buying and selling organs. If the cognitive-death definition were instituted, organ merchandising corporations might establish an enterprise beyond Wall Street's wildest dreams. The world would find itself in a society where death itself would be a business.

CHAPTER 8

RELIGION IS A MAN-MADE DESIGN IN ORDER TO PUT FEAR AND CONTROL THE MASSES

Religion was created for the purpose to control and put fear in the people. Leaders did this as a way to manipulate the masses, so they could gain power over them.

The foundation behind religion is that if you commit sin, you will go to hell. These manipulators' will put this mess in your head that unless you live by a certain set of rules, they are going to hell. The truth is that hell doesn't exist, is nothing more than a state of mind, hell is what you go through and heaven is what you make it. But like religion, hell is a made up ideal to scare people into following a set of rules in order to keep societies under control.

I'm amazed on how people are still gullible enough to fall for this crap. I believe that religion is for people who can't think for themselves and has no individuality, so they simply join a religion and allow that religion to control their thinking.

The only people who benefit from religion are the religion leaders. How many gullible people have paid money to the church, these preachers, and pastors who are no different than door to door salesman, they like to teach the poor lies and say that the Almighty God is a spook in the sky that you can't see with the physical eye. They are like a bunch of crack dealers who had traded in their dope for hope, and turn around and sold it to you.

Religion also forces people to deny their true nature. Things like no sex before marriage etc... Yet we are sexual beings and sex is a perfectly normal and natural thing.

The way to move forward is to become a free-thinking, free willed individual and to think for yourself and live life on your own terms. To pursue your own happiness and personal goals and not blindly following a made up religion and advocating you're thinking to that religion.

As long as you don't hurt anyone or do anything illegal in society, you can do whatever you want. You're not going to hell' or any of that nonsense.

Religion is the cause of most war and conflict in the world. Without religion, we all could get along a lot better. So people it's time to rid yourself of religion and become a free thinking human being instead.

CHAPTER 9

WHAT THEY REALLY DIDN'T
TELL YOU ABOUT 9/11

Right before the 9/11 attacks happen, some sneaky business took place within the stock market and insurance firms. An extraordinary amount of options were placed on United Airlines and American Airlines stocks, the same airlines that were hijacked during the attacks. There is a saying that the traders were tipped off about the attacks and profited from the tragedy.

WHY DIDN'T THE AIR DEFENSE SHOOT DOWN THE PLANES?

In the event that an airplane were to be hijacked, the North American Aerospace Defense Command (NORAD) is prepared to send out fighters jets which can debilitate or shoot down an airplane. On 9/11 NORAD generals did know of the hijackings in time to scramble fighter jets. It is said that NORAD commanded defense systems was down, and this was the reason for the lack of presence during the attacks.

WAS IT BOMBS THAT REALLY TOOK DOWN THE TOWERS?

The World Trade Center collapse appeared similar to a control annihilation. It is said that the towers were in fact blown down with explosives placed in selected locations. Some witnesses accounted hearing explosions inside the building as they attempted to escape. Many architects and sciences even maintained that a planes fuel cannot produce enough heat to melt the steel frame of the two buildings that collapsed.

THE PUZZLING ATTACK ON THE PENTAGON:

The Pentagon crash may be the most puzzling event of them all. I think that the impact holes in the Pentagon were much smaller than a commercial American Allies plane. I also question why the plane was not shot down prior to impact as well as why the plane impacted into a section of the Pentagon that was vacant due to renovations.

FLIGHT 93 WAS A COMPLETE SETUP:

The fourth hijacked plane, flight 93, crashed in Shanksville, Pennsylvania. It is said that the passengers fought back and crashed the plane into a field. They could have landed safely, while a substitute plane was shot out of the sky. I believe that the passengers were murdered or relocated and will never be found ever.

IS IT TRUE THAT THE HIJACKERS ARE STILL ALIVE?

After the September 11 attacks, the "Loose Change" documentary stated that all of the hijackers were in fact alive in other countries. Rather presumptuous since it is possible for two different people to have identical names. But they did raise a good point; how did the passports of the terrorist survived the explosion? In the aftermath of the attacks, passports and identifications were found as evidence. So I asked the question, how do your ID that is made out of paper survived an explosion which destroyed buildings.

WAS THERE PHONE CALLS MADE ON THE PLANE?

They said there where phone calls made on the planes. But it's a fact that a cell phone cannot receive reception from the altitude that planes normally fly at. And it was said that a phone call was made by a boy to his mother, in which he referred to himself by his first and last name.

DID SOME OF THE PEOPLE KNEW ABOUT THE ATTACKS BEFORE IT HAPPEN, AND TOOK OFF WORK?

They said that 4,000 employees took off from work on 9/11. Some of the first people to record the attacks on camera were employees also. Police became suspicious of their actions and put them on the radar as suspects in the wake of the attacks.

BLACK BOXES WERE FOUND, AND WAS KEPT A SECRET.

During the following days after the attacks, the black boxes were one of the most important items to find. They were the only evidence into what happened inside the cockpit of the planes. Three of the four boxes were found and only one was in good enough condition to listen too. The tape was not originally released but was shared with the families a year later. I believe the tapes were not revealed in order to support their scheme.

I THINK THAT THE BIN LADEN VIDEOS WHERE PHONY

Truthfully, Bin Laden denied any responsibility or involvement with the attacks. Soon afterward, several videos came out claiming that he took full responsibility for the attacks. I think that old Bin was targeted because of his stakes in the stocks as well as former President George Bush personal business projects in the so-called Middle East.

HOW COULD ALUMINUM PLANES GO THROUGH A STEEL STRUCTURE?

Commercial airplanes frames are constructed with a very light aluminum material in order to make it easier to fly. I have studied that there is no possible way that an airplane can do as much damage as it did to the Twin Towers as it did. I have a strong belief that missiles or explosives were used to ensure that the buildings fall.

CHAPTER 10

THE LICENSES SCHEME

Wow! Where should I start? Well let me begin by saying that the authority to license, if any such authority can be said to exist, is the power to control, regulate, stifle, intimidate, rob and or destroy an individual or an organization of individuals and their activities or products. Licensing is the ugly fist of protectionism, suited better to a dictatorship than to a free republic. Governments are fond of licensing, as evidenced by all manner of secretaries, boards and commissions whose function is to oversee such things and assure government an additional source of revenue from the price of granting its permission. Tyrannical governments prefer that their subjects or slaves be required to ask for their permission prior to, and as a condition of doing nearly every kind of public, private or independent activity. Such governments want servile subjects who do what they are told to do. Therefore the necessity of making an acceptance of licensing, as being "for the common good" or for public protection.

A review of the prohibitions, requirements and options of the government under our constitutional contract is revealing. Nowhere can there be found any general option or requirement for government to license anything or anyone except in article 1, section 8, wherein Congress was given the option to regulate commerce with foreign nations.

It is important to remember that the Constitution is a contract of limitations on government. It is a prescription for exactly what government shall or may do and how it shall or may proceed, and it specifies the specific purpose of such government as shall rightfully exist. The six purposes given in the opening of the Constitution are offended by any government sponsored licensing activities. Government licensing creates injustice and makes tranquility and liberty insecure.

The whole question of government licensing is centered on the difference between a right and a privilege. A free individual may choose to do anything as long there's no threat or harm is done to the life, liberty or property of another individual. Those with the courage to claim an exercise their rights as re-affirmed in the Constitution do so with the concurrence of the highest law of the land, that it is their right as a free people to do so.

You shouldn't have to get permission to exercise a right but one does have to ask and obtain permission to use or do something which transgresses the rights or property of another. In such a case the one owning the right, or piece of property as the case may be, is the only one with sufficient authority to grant another person any kind of permission or privilege. Since the government must protect everyone equally and cannot properly favor anyone with its gratuities and since government has no rights, but only duties and requirements with options and prohibition for fulfilling them, and since constitutionally speaking, government does not have the authority to collect any revenues other than those resulting from property laid taxes, duties, or possibly fines due from criminal convictions. The government has no authority to profit financially from licensing, thousands of people have claimed their natural birth right to liberty and have various types of licenses. These anti-bureaucratic forms have two purposes, one to claim their rights in a responsible and organized way as a peaceful transitional declaratory offering for government observance, and to introduce the freedom movement and the concept of liberty to others.

IS DRIVING A CAR ON THE ROAD, A RIGHT OR PRIVILEGE?

Here is an argument that has been raging on for years. There are so-called sovereign individuals who carry constitutional driver license or right to travel cards and refused to be brought under the police power or the jurisdiction of the state while in the normal course of driving. Now are these individuals practicing civil disobedience on general principle? Are these people just out of their mind, or have they got a valid case? Well let's take a look at the issue here.

Case law tells us what the courts have decided in issues about "right vs privilege" In the case of Chicago Motor Coach vs Chicago, 169 NE 22; and in 25 American Jurisprudence (1st) Highways Sect. 163, we will find that. "The use of the highways for the purpose of travel and transportation is not a mere privilege, but a common and fundamental right of which the public and individual cannot be rightfully deprived." So here we have a court cases and a quote from one of our basic American law volumes telling us that we have an absolute right to use the roadways.

The case of Thompson vs Smith, 154 SE 579 found: "The right of the citizen to travel upon the public highways and to transport his property thereon, either by horse drawn carriage or by automobile, is not a mere privilege which a city can prohibit or permit at will, but a common right which he has under the right to life, liberty and the pursuit of happiness."

On the other hand, those who use the roadways for profit and business rather than for personal reasons, are exercising an extraordinary use. This extraordinary use of public roadways is a privilege, so if you have a trucking business, or if you are running a transportation service, etc. then the state has a right to license and regulate your activities upon the roadways.

Now, if we had the right to drive our automobiles (by definition, the law holds that an automobile is used for pleasure and/or personal use whereas a motor vehicle is used for commercial purposes on our roadways. Then why do we need a license? Most people think that getting a driver's license is a way for the state to determine competency, and primarily it does work that way but if that was the only reason, then regular testing would be in order rather than just a renewal fee every several years. Furthermore, here's something else to think about, if licensing by the state proved competency, wouldn't the state be somehow liable for accidents caused by incompetent drivers? But no matter how responsibility is parceled out, the fact remains that a license indicates that the activity is a privilege. By definition, it is permission to do something that would be otherwise illegal. The only way to turn a right into a privilege and place the individual into a commercial category is to have the individual waive his/her right.

So who in their right mind would waive a right and deliberately place themselves under the police power and state regulations? No one! That's why we were never told that when we first signed our names to our driver's licenses, we effectively signed away our Constitutional and legal rights. In other words, you contracted (an "unrevealed" contract) with the state to be treated like a commercial entity. If you were not told that then you were the victim of constructive fraud.

STATE LAWS

While motor vehicle laws vary from state to state, the application of those laws is often done in a deceptive manner. I used New Jersey's title 39 -- the motor vehicles code -- as an example. In their book Chapter 3, paragraph 1 say:

Certain vehicles excepted from chapter: Automobile fire engines and such self-propelling vehicles as are used neither for the conveyance of persons for hire, pleasure or business, nor for the transportation of freights, such as stream road rollers and traction engines are excepted from the provisions of this chapter.

The language that was just mention is rather clumsy, but basically it means that if you're not using your car, van or truck for commercial purposes, then you are exempted from that chapter. The rest of the chapter consists of registration and licensing requirements, which the above paragraph states, applies only to vehicles used in commerce.

Again, in Title V of the vehicle and traffic laws of the State of New York, which govern drivers licenses, we find that under article 18,

Paragraph 500, says, *"except as otherwise expressly provided in this chapter, this title shall be exclusively controlling: a. upon licensing and regulation of drivers; and b, on their use of public* highways.

One of the prime reasons for the misunderstanding regarding who is subject to these statues is the use of the terms "motor vehicle" and "driver." Both of these terms are "commercial" that is legally a "motor vehicle" which is used for commerce, like a taxi or for the transportation of goods, as opposed to an "automobile" which is used for personal reasons, going to and from work, going shopping etc. a driver is what we everyday folks would call a chauffeur or one who drives a vehicle for hire. So if you agree that you are a driver of a motor vehicle, then you are putting yourself into a commercial class subject to regulations and statues.

Now try to read the legal material above again. Now in light of your new understanding of the words "motor vehicle" and "driver." It's a whole different ball game!

So when words are used in such a manner to confuse people they are called "wordplay." The Internal Revenue Service is famous for this. How would anybody know that the word "income" has been ruled by the Supreme Court to mean, profit or a gain," as when you earn interest or extra from an investment or rent out real estate. Exchanging your labor for money is compensation, but all of that is another subject.

The moment you buy it from the manufacture! The states fraudulent actions begins as soon as a motor vehicle or automobile is purchased from the manufacture. If you have a problem believing that you are a victim of fraud by the state, then just read on.

"Paramount Title" is the highest evidence of ownership. It is also known as a Manufacturers Certificate of Origin or (MCO) or a (MSO) which means Manufacturers Statement of Origin, depending on which state is setting the caption. These instruments are more negotiable than the Certificate of Title, which is what we wind up with. Under the licensing agreements set between the car dealer and the DMV agency, at the time of the original sale of the automobile, the MSO is appropriated by the DMV. This is done without disclosing the nature of the transaction to the original buyer who pays the considerations for the purchase. The state who gets the negotiable instrument which the buyer just paid for, then puts the Paramount Title on microfilm. The originals are destroyed. This sets in motion an incredibly lucrative revenue generating machine for the state.

So apparently, the DMV agencies through their parent agencies, The Dep's of Transportation use these harsh gotten properties as collateral against which bonds are generated to finance highway work projects and probably other state activities too.

THE REGISTRATION SCAM

Now back in the day, when registering motorized transportations became a requirement, the registration process was sold to the people as a safety precaution. Should the vehicle get stolen, it made it easier for the authorities to recover it for you. As we approach the year 2016 just add up all the taxes, fees and surcharges you've ever paid on your car, you would think that you'd be better off taking your chances with the crack heads trying to steal your car on the streets

Since we now know that the state swindles the people of their ownership of their vehicles when it's sold, we see that our yearly registration fees are in fact, leasing fees! In many states, registration renewal is set at a percentage of the automobile's current value.

So the fact is that the vehicles that we drive are all leased, and the people that leased it to you has the right to set the rules that you must follow while using the leasing states property. In other words if we violate the rules of the road we have no right to complain about the tickets we receive because by registering with the state, we have all agreed to accept this mess. The fact that we were tricked into doing so has to be addressed, and it should begin with our legislators. They are hired to pass laws that are beneficial to us, not to conspire with the state to suck the people dry for their hard earned money.

Now as long as the focus of this book has turned to the people we've put in power supposedly to protect us from harm, here's another point to consider. Across America, drive's education is taught in just about all of the high schools. This is a subject I haven't researched, so if I'm wrong then so be it, but I don't think any of the above-mentioned regarding our so-called freedom of mobility is even thought about, much less brought up as a topic for discussion in any of the public schools. On that basis, it would seem that the education community is also in cahoots with the state, and why not? Because our tax dollars funds the school system, but the money is first laundered through the state. From the mouth of the founder of the European banking family Mayer Rothschild. *"Allow me to hold the purse strings and I care not who makes the laws."*

TAXES AND MORE TAXES

Now, consider what happens when we sell our cars. The original buyer pays a sales tax, but when we decide to pass it along to someone else, that person pays a sales tax again. And when that "owner" wants to sell it, the following owner will pay yet another sales tax, and on and on. We are at a loss to think of any other item upon which sales tax is paid over and over again. Think about it, how did the state survived before cars were invented? Just asking!

CHAPTER 11

THE AMERICAN BANKRUPTCY

The U.S. Congress was charged with the responsibility of managing the U.S. finances in Article 1 section 8 clause 5 of the

U.S. Constitution and Article 1 section 10 of the United States Constitution. That said, states may not coin their own money nor make anything but gold and silver coin for tender in payment of debts.

The U.S. Congress is supposed to be responsible for the financial affairs of the U.S. and not the privately owned and operated Federal Reserve which functions as the Un-Constitutional central bank of the United States. Now I have found out that 52% of this is owned by Rothschild Bank of London and Berlin; 8% owned by Lazard Frères Bank of Paris, and also Israel Moses of Serif Bank in Italy who own 8% just to name a few.

When the U.S. bankruptcy of 1930 was declared in the U.S. Congress in 1933, gold was taken out of circulation and the Un-Constitutional fraudulent U.S. currency made its debut. All of the fraudulent U.S. currency in circulation is made at an average rate of two cents per dollar, that's about what they are worth regardless of domination. The United States treasury sells these bills to the Federal Reserve at cost.

Whenever the United States government needs a loan, the United States treasury borrows those same bills from the Federal

Reserve at face value plus interest and the American people gets taxed to pay the face value, plus the interest to the owners of the Federal Reserve by the privately owned and operated collection agency known as the Internal Racketeering Squad. Any American citizen that has ever allegedly paid the IRS should look at who endorsed the check used for payment (it was not the U.S. Treasury so the American people can forget about their taxes being used for running the country). You cannot pay debt with debt. You can only pay a debt with substance. The fraudulent U.S. dollar is a tender (a fancy way of saying I. O. U) that has no material value {Give me a pound, a pound of what?} On the back of the American currency you will find not one seal but two. These two seals depict two different governments, with two different jurisdictions. Unless you were a Mason. Most Americans had never seen the Great Seal, it's the Pyramid with the all Seeing Eye, prior to the late 1920s.

What are they telling the American people by having this seal on the back of their medium of exchange?

They are telling the people that the United States is beholden to their lenders, due to the outstanding loan that has to be repaid.

Now back to the subject of bankruptcy. There have been no chartered banks in the United States venue since the inception of the U.S. bankruptcy in 1933. With gold pulled out of circulation, banks in the United States venue began loaning commercial instruments in place of money/substance which translates as they loan you nothing and charge you interest which is usury. This is the true inspiration behind all gun control laws. They know that when the unsuspecting so-called citizens of America finally figure out that they were sold out, the armed radical people of United States will come after them with their guns blazing.

The Federal Reserve is used on the American citizens [Technically, there is no such thing as a U.S. citizen because the United States is a for-profit corporation chartered to business that has sub diaries (STATE OF NEW MEXICO as supposed to the New – Mexico – State: Republic) and franchises(U.S. citizen/resident aliens/artificial entities/corporations/you have no rights that a court is bound to respect because as an inanimate object before a court, you have no feelings, cannot own anything, cannot speak thus cannot state a claim upon which relief may be granted, because if that was the case, the for profit corporation

"Mc Donald's" could make you a citizen/have its own citizenry.] while the International Monetary Fund and World Bank are used on the people in Kenya, Zimbabwe, Indonesia, Korea, etc. The I.M.F. and World Bank suckered these governments into accepting loans of nothing [fraudulent/nonexistent U.S. currency] and charged them interest. In turn, these governments (Like their U.S. citizen counterparts) voluntarily elected into the fraud unknowingly and pledged to repay the non-loan [Hey! I'm good for it] as they pledged all of the labor of their respective citizenry and all that they own including their sovereignty thus their citizenry became a surety/ collateral that backs the securities sold to the highest bidder every business day on what is called the bond market. So congratulations!!! You've just been pawned.

I like to say this one more thing before I close this chapter. That this is why the U. N. is demanding that its members make all of their citizens have a birth certificate. The registered birth certificate is tied to a surety/collateral/laborer/you [There is a bond attached to the birth certificate that is sold on the bond market also] that will be taxed to pay the non-loan and interest. Suckered hook line and sinker.

CHAPTER 12

WHAT IS A BRITH CERTIFICATE

A birth certificate is a (Bond) that is issued by the state, and are collateral instruments/mortgages, and are a deceptive method which places your child in bondage. So that child service agencies are able to chattel the children at will. You must understand that at the point of birth your child is robbed from you by the corporate state, and are enslaved as fictitious, (strawman), corporate entities.

These instruments are used as collateral, through negotiable bank bonds for corporate profit. These bonds are systematically fractionalized to create greater profit. This creates the massive deficit.

THIS IS INSTITUTIONALIZED, BUREAUCRATIZED ENSLAVEMENT!

The fact that many Americans are becoming conscious of what is really going on has contributed greatly to the fall of the corporations, the fall of the democracy of which the people have

90

thought is the proper government authority, when it is not. It is as it states demo – craft, inferior. It is stated in the supreme law of the land so-called Constitution, that the supreme law is guaranteed as a Republic (which is a Matriarch).

Now as I was saying before, your child is held as ward property deemed as state chattel. Under ward - ship tenures the child is claimed by the foreign fictitious corporate entity, called "THE STATE COLONY." The states are the bond holders of titles, birth records/certificates, marriage certificates, and driver's licenses, etc. As negotiable bond holdings, binding you and your child as the lien.

This deceptive activity occurs with your unconscious actions, through your unknowing yet willing consent. Now if you are concern about your child warfare you must take action against this, and that is not to except the chattel bondage instrument/birth certificate which gives the elite the contractual right to chattel you and your children. Yet, the birth certificate is not really a contract. It does not pass the definition of a lawful contract. So to stop using it is important. By cutting your connection voids the contract, although many may want to dissolve it in writing, as it is a corporate commercial instrument. By continuing to use it, you are agreeing and making it valid upon you and your child by your own admission.

You will also find disturbing to know how an administrative procedure can remove your child from your home. In 1921 Congress passed the (Sheppard Towner Maternity Act) that created the United States birth "registration" area (see public law 97, 67th Congress, session 1, chapter 135, 1921.) That act allows you to register your child when they are born. If you do so, you will get a copy of the birth certificate. By registering your child, which is voluntary, they become federal property. Which does several things, your child become subjects of Congress (they lose their state citizenship). A copy of the birth certificate is sent to the department of vital statistics in the state in which they were born. The original birth certificate is sent to the Department of Commerce in the District of Columbia. It is then forwarded to an International Monetary Fund IMF building in Europe. Your child's future labor and properties are put up as collateral for the nation's debt.

So to sum this up, all of us who are legally within this nation will be treated as criminals, tracked and monitored by the computers and programs, and as aliens subject to taxes created by international treaty, or imposed by statute upon same and keeping with the original taxation and government funding scheme of the United States Constitution.

CHAPTER 13

THE MARK OF THE BEAST, IT'S ALREADY HERE.

For the last 15 years I have told many people that their social security number is the "Mark of the Beast." Now I'm not a religious person, nor is I'm associated with any superstition organization called religion, but I can say that I'm a realist, meaning that I can see things for what it is. And that is Americans can't get a job, get a driver's license, have a bank account, get a loan, vote, or even file a tax return without the "Mark of the Beast" a.k.a. "Social Security Number." The elite/the devils knows what you make, what you have, and where to find you. They just might kill me for writing this book but that's another subject so let me continue. Next will come fingerprinting and electronic banking which is already here. You will not be able to purchase food or medicine for yourself or your family without the "Mark/Security Number." Your child will be (which is already happening) raised and schooled by the beast/devil. Now the police, and the federal monitors in the schools reports your child's every move, I challenge you to name a single area of your physical life not controlled by the government. The technology exists to put your life information on a chip, which is similar to the magnetic strip on a credit card and to implant the chip under the skin. There is already talk in Washington of using implants in the U.S. military for identification purposes. Will the rest of America be next?

Don't believe it? What I just said is just an example, let me break down the proof. Now they say that 666 is a number of a man. And it is man who is responsible for all the rights and wrongs in the world, and since mathematics is the universal language it's the foundation in which all things are made. Now nine is the highest number in mathematics. And since man is the highest form in creation, nine is his signature birth mark. For example, man has

94

nine holes in his body, it takes nine months for a woman to give birth, and we have nine planets in our solar system, still not convinced. Well let's look at the number 666, if you add them up 6+6+6 = 18 1+8 = you get 9. Now let's flip the numbers around 999, 9+9+9 =27 2+7 = also 9. Do you get the picture now, this is not a coincidence and the people who are doing this are not stupid. They are not going to put this mark right in your face for you to see, they are not going to speak to you in English or in any other language but mathematics, if you notice that the Supreme Court has nine judges. Now let's take the English alphabet which has 26 letters and ends with the number six. It says in the Bible that man was made on the sixth day, so why is this, what is the connection between man and the numbers six and nine, well I'll tell you. First I need you to get a blank sheet of paper and write down the alphabet from A to Z and multiply each letter by six, for example:

6   12   18

A   b   c

Once you have wrote this down like it's written from A though Z, multiply each letter by six, you should come out with the number 156, which also ends with the number six. Now we all know that whenever we buy or sale something in corporate America, or do anything that requires you giving up your information. It goes in that big belly beast called the computer. Now what I'm about to tell you is going to shock you so I need you to pay attention. Now after you have wrote down the alphabet and have match the numbers with the letters, next I need you to write down the word computer. Just like I have it down at the bottom.

C   18

O

M

P

U

T

E

R

Now find the number that is above C which is 18, now once you have matched the numbers with the letters in the word computer, you would see the number you will come out with. I'm not going to tell you what the number is, I wanted you to see it for yourself. And once you have, I want you to remember that your social security number has nine numbers that is always being typed in a computer.

The formula that I have just mentioned is one of many examples, this mark is already controlling your life. The Constitution of America no longer exists, federal courts operate under international law, the bill of rights are gone, the states have no rights, and you don't have no rights! What I'm saying is labeled as hate talk and may not have the freedom to say it much longer. Since I hate tyranny, I am considered dangerous by the government. Also the non-government organization, and environmentalist groups supported by the elite, the lifestyle of your family will forever change.

CHAPTER 14

THE WEAPON OF HURRICANE KATRINA

Just about every man, woman and child in American is totally unaware that technology exists NOW! Whereby weather can be used as a Weapon of Mass Destruction. And that weapon is called Tesla's Scalar technology, which is being used by the U.S., Russia, Japan and possibly other countries. Since the people have not been made aware of this amazing technology, the elite who control the world's major governments, can use scalar technology for profit without being detected by the six billion people on planet earth.

Now what you was told all over the airwaves after Hurricane Katrina was that the cost of oil was going to go way up. The hurricane was being blamed for the much higher prices of oil that caused one of the worse economy catalysts in American history, which the elite had planned for their personal financial benefit. It was no accident that Bush, Cheney, Rice etc., all happen to be connected to the House of Saudis and the oil conglomerates. The Afghani and Iraqi wars are all worth trillions of dollars of oil in those regions.

The elite and their government agents, Bush, Blair, Cheney, Rice, Putin, Sharon to name several, they all play their roles in the elite's hideous plan to control the entire world. They do not care or have any compassion for the millions of Americans who will

98

have to be killed for the elite to achieve their sick agenda. Hurricane Katrina and the destruction and suffering it has caused is just one example of how far they will go, working behind the scenes manipulating these catastrophic wars and events on their way to achieve what they call their 'Great Work of Ages."

Bush and Cheney and the elite posse and their connected associates all benefitted financially from Hurricane Katrina to the tune of hundreds of billions and over the long term, trillion of dollars. They reap the huge profits from higher oil prices. They received billions of dollars in contracts to rebuild New Orleans and all the other areas devastated by this storm. They were able to buy the devastated property for pennies on the dollar. Their banks received huge amounts of interest on the loans that was made out to the U.S. government, corporations and individuals who needed the financing for rebuilding. This same code of destroy and rebuild plan for profit was used in WW I and WW II and is currently being used in Afghanistan and Iraq.

THE US MILITARY'S EXPERIMENTS WITH CLIMATIC WARFARE

People in America don't know that the world's weather can now be modified as an electromagnetic weapon. Both the U.S. and China have developed capabilities to manipulate the climate for military use.

Environmental modification techniques have been applied by the U.S. military for more than fifty years. A mathematician by the name John Neumann who worked with the US Department of Defense, started his research on weather modification in the late 1940s at the height of the Cold War, and foresaw 'forms of climatic warfare as yet at that time seem unimaginable. During the Vietnam War, cloud seeding techniques were used, starting in 1967 under Project Popeye, the objective of which was to prolong the monsoon season and block enemy supply routes along the Ho Chi Minh Trail.

WHAT IS HAARP AND WHAT DOES IT DO?

The US military has developed advanced capabilities that enable it selectively to alter weather patterns. The technology which is being perfected under the high frequency activity auroral research program called (HAARP). It is an appendage of strategic defense Initiative – Star Wars. From a military standpoint, HAARP is a weapon of mass destruction, operating from the outer atmosphere and capable of destabilizing agricultural and ecological systems around the world.

Whether modification according to the US Air Force document AF 2025 Final Report, offers the war fighter a wide range of possible options to defeat any adversary, to the extent of triggering floods, hurricanes, droughts and earthquakes. Whether modification will become a part of domestic and international security and could be done unilaterally. It could have offensive and defensive applications and even be used for deterrence purposes. The ability to generate precipitation, fog and storms on earth or to modify space weather. And the production of artificial weather are all part of an integrated set of military technologies.

CHAPTER 15

THE CREATION OF THE AIDS VIRUS

ST. JOHN THE BAPTIST PARISH LIBRARY
2920 NEW HIGHWAY 51
LAPLACE, LOUISIANA 70068

If you believe the government propaganda that AIDS is incurable then you are going to die even sooner than the rest of us. The common cold is a virus. Have you ever had a cold? How did you catch it? You don't really know do you? If the cold virus were fatal how many people would there be left in the world?

Now yellow fever is a virus. You catch it from mosquito bites. Malaria is a parasite also carried by mosquitoes. It is many times larger than the AIDS virus (it's like comparing a knife to a machete) yet the mosquito easily carries this virus to people.

The tuberculosis germ, also much bigger than the AIDS virus, can be transmitted by towels, blanket's, etc. The AIDS virus can live for as long as 10 days on a dry glass. You can't understand this murder mystery unless you learn a little virology.

First you need to know that many viruses grow in animals and many grow in humans, but most of the viruses that affect animals don't affect humans. There are exception of course such as yellow fever and small pox.

There are some viruses in animals that cause very lethal cancer in them, but do not effect man. The bovine leukemia virus, for example is lethal to cows but not humans. There is another virus that occurs in sheep called sheep visna virus which is also non –reactive in people. These deadly viruses are "retro viruses" meaning that they can change the genetic composition of cells that they enter.

The World Health Organization had published an article calling for scientists to work with these deadly causes and try to make a hybrid virus that would be deadly to people. Now why would they want to do this? Is it even remotely possible that the World Health Organization would want to develop a virus that would wipe out the world? What I believe is if these developments worked, then many terrible and fatal infectious viruses could be made even more terrible than anyone could imagine.

Many people believe in conspiracies and many don't. Is there a conspiracy to kill off half the population? Well this debate still continues, and people keep changing their minds. One day it's no, the next day it's yes, depending on what's on the news or who said what on YouTube.

But it doesn't take a bad News report to see the connection between the U.S. government and the AIDS pandemic. But what about the green monkey? Some of the best virologist in the world and many of those directly involved in the AIDS research have said that the green monkey may be the culprit or that it started in the gay community. We all know the stories, one was that a green monkey bit an Africa on the ass and boom! AIDS all over the place.

Now I don't know about you, but anybody with any common sense will know this sounds absolutely stupid. Now any virologist know that the AIDs virus doesn't occur naturally in monkeys. In fact it doesn't occur naturally in any animal. AIDS started practically simultaneously in Africa, Europe, America, and all over. So tell me was this green monkey flying around in all these places?) Examination of the gene structure of the green monkey cells proves that it is not genetically possible to transfer the AIDS virus from monkeys to man by natural means. Because of the artificial nature of the AIDS virus it will not easily transfer from man to man until it has become very concentrated in the body fluids through repeated injections from person to person such as drug addicts, and through high multiple sexual partners and among homosexuals. After repeated transfer it can become a natural infection for man, which is the case now.

A man by the name of Dr. Theodore Stretcher's indicates that the National Cancer Institute in collaboration with the World Health Organization made the AIDS virus in their laboratories at Fort Detrick (now NCI). They combined the deadly retroviruses, bovine leukemia virus and sheep visna virus, and injected them into human tissue. The result was the AIDS virus, the first human retrovirus known to man and now believed to be 100% fatal to those effected.

So now the green monkey theory can be thrown out the window and the more logical explanation for the AIDS virus can be blamed on the real villains, and that is the government elite. Which are in the process of conducting germ warfare from Fort Detrick against the free world, especially the United States, even using foreign communist agents within the United States Army germ warfare unit indirectly called the Army Infectious Disease Unit.

Now can you imagine that? A devil in the biological warfare center with the full blessing of the U.S. government. The creation of the AIDS virus by these evil people was not just a diabolical scientific exercise that got out of hand. It was a cold-blooded

105

successful attempt to create a killer virus which was then used in a successful experiment in Africa. So successful in fact that most of central Africa may be wiped out, 100,000,000 dead within the next ten years.

The people must understand this isn't an accident. This was done deliberately, in the Federation Proceedings of the United States in 1972 it was said that in the relations to the immune response a number of useful experimental approaches can be visualized. Meaning that they suggested a way to put their new killer virus out into the world by using a vaccination program, and then sit back and observe the results. That is, give the AIDS virus to the brothers and sisters and see if they die, who dies first, and of what, just like using rats in a laboratory.

They used smallpox vaccine for their vehicle and the geographical sites chosen in 1972 were Uganda and other African states, Haiti, Brazil and Japan. The present or recent past of AIDS epidemiology coincides with these geographical areas.

So the point is, if the African green monkey could transmit AIDS to humans the present know amount of infections in Africa makes it statistically impossible for a single episode, such as a

106

monkey biting someone, to have brought this epidemic to this point. The doubling time of the number of people infected, about every 14 months, when correlated with the first known case, and the present known number of cases prove beyond a doubt that a large number of people had to have been infected at the same time.

Beginning in 1972 with the first so – called case from a fairy tale monkey that doubled the number infected from a single source every 2 years, you get only a few thousand cases. From 1972 to 1987 is 15 years or 180 months. If it takes 2 years to double the number of cases then there would have been 13 doublings, 1 then 2, then 4 then 8, etc. So in 15 years, from a single source of infection there would be about 8,000 cases in Africa, and not 75 million AIDS infected people. We are approaching World War III here without a shot being fired.

So why did the experts on the AIDS virus keep talking about green monkeys and gays being the culprits when it was obvious that AIDS was a man-made virus? Did they say that it was a homosexual or a drug user disease, when in Africa it's more Pro-heterosexual there? If the green monkey did it then why did AIDS explode practically simultaneously in Africa and everywhere else? When it was proposed to the National Institute of Health that the AIDS virus was a combination of two bovine or sheep viruses cultured in human cells in a laboratory, did they say it was "bad science" when that's exactly what occurred.

There are 9,000 base pairs on the genome. Some will cause brain rot similar to the sheep virus, some leukemia-like diseases from the cow virus and some that won't do anything. Because of the multiple of possible combinations of viruses that makes up the AIDS disease, it will never be a vaccine. Even if they did develop a vaccine they would undoubtedly give us something equally bad as they did with the polio vaccine (cancer of the brain), the swine flu vaccine (a polio-like disease), the smallpox vaccine (AIDS), and the hepatitis vaccine (AIDS).

There was an article written by the Centers for Disease Control in 1981 stating that four percent of those receiving the hepatitis-vaccine were AIDS affected. In 1984 they admitted to 60 percent. Now they refused to give out figures at all because they don't want to admit that 100 percent of hepatitis vaccine receivers are affected with AIDS. Where is the data on the hepatitis vaccine studies? With the FDA? CDC? No, the US Department of Justice has it put away so you would never see it. What has the government told us about AIDS?

(1). It's a gay man disease-which was a lie.

(2). It is related to unclean sex-which was a lie.

(3). only a small percentage of those testing positive for HIV would not get the disease-which was a lie.

(4). It came from the African green back monkey-which was a lie.

(5). It was due to popping needles with drug addicts-which was a lie.

(6). It started 400 years ago by the Portuguese-which was a lie. (It was only discovered in 1972).

(7). you can't get it from mosquito bites-which was a lie.

(8). the virus can't live outside the body-which is another lie.

Now as I have pointed out, the AIDS virus is a human disease. Whether the infection of 75 million Africans was deliberate or accidental, which I don't think was a mistake but can be debated. There is absolutely no scientific evidence that this laboratory virus was present in Africa before the World Health Organization descended upon those helpless people in 1967 with their deadly

109

AIDS-laced vaccine. The AIDS virus didn't come from Africa, but from Fort Detrick, Maryland U.S.A

CHAPTER 16

FACEBOOK OR FAKEBOOK?
IS IT A GOVERNMENT WATCH DOG

Now we're faced with the very possible that Facebook has a direct relationship with the federal government and that it may even be involved as a source of data mining for the government. During the past couple years it's been publicized that these data mining and surveillance programs do exist. For example the wiretapping and surveillance project, no longer does the Facebook/Government relationship seem like a theory anymore.

My opinion if you are a Facebook freak and you like putting as much information on its site. Facebook goes as far as to ask you for everything from movies interests, job history, hometown, phone numbers, email, clubs, sexual orientation, etc. Again, this is why I don't have a Facebook. I'm not a glutton for attention. I don't have to have that mess, and I'm sure not going to put all my personal information on a social screen for every Tom, Dick, and Harry to see.

Another aspect is that a lot of people don't know is that employers are starting to use Facebook to screen potential employees. Your next job could be lost or gained based on your Facebook profiles. Scary is it? You bet. Law enforcement has even begun to use Facebook as a source of information, clues, and leads in ongoing investigation and potential threats. So your privacy may be at far greater risk of being violated than you know. The site had been under fire before, charging for the site, and among other things, manipulates privacy settings to make users' personal information available for commercial use. Also, some Facebook users found their private chats available to everyone on their contact list, a major security breach that's left a lot of people wondering just how secure the site is.

There are all kinds of ways that people can access information about you. For instance, you may not realize that when you are playing the popular games on Facebook, such as Farmville, or take those popular quizzes. Every time you do that you authorize an application to be downloaded to your profile that gives information to a third party about you that you have never signed off on, and that my friend is a scary thought.

Now the big question about who owns Facebook is another subject because in today's world of advanced modern technology, there are billions of people that use the Internet as a means of communication. The era of Big Brother is upon us. Now everyday just walking down the road for a burger, our faces are recorded on numerous of cameras. Even while waiting for your burgers to cook, your image is being burned elsewhere.

You got to understand that our society is a paranoid one, and rightly so. We are never really alone. Business' record every keystroke and every action in an employee's day. International Intelligence agencies scan and flag any messages containing certain buzz words. Why? Because the truth is out there!"

The question has been raised that Facebook has connection with the CIA. And the reason that might be is because Facebook has a resource that any secret intelligence agency in the world would die for.

A site that has access to over 70 million people names, addresses, friends, activities, details about them, even phone numbers and emails.

Given the CIA's shady past and reputation for doing anything to get information they need (You've seen the news, torture, abuse, abductions, you name it). You would consider that at least one secret agency would attempt to contact Facebook, the fastest growing social networking website in the world. Facebook may also collect information about you from other sources, such as newspapers, blogs, instant messaging services, and other users of the Facebook service through the operation of the service such as photo tags in order to provide you with more useful information and a more personalized experience.

By using Facebook you are consenting to have your personal data transferred to and processed in the United States. When you use Facebook you may set up your personal profile, form relationships, send messages, perform searches and queries, form groups, set up events, add applications, and transmit information through various channels.

113

They also use information about you that they collect from other sources, including retail sites, Facebook platform developers and other users of Facebook to supplement your profile.

After Facebook was created by so-called Harvard drop-out Mark Zuckerberg in 2004, and became a success. It got the attention of venture capitalist Peter Thiel, founder and former CEO of Paypal. He invested a little over $500,000, which really got Facebook off its feet. Facebook's first angel investors appear to be connected to the Central intelligence Agency, A.K.A. CIA.

So see everything is interconnected. Everything is related. DARPA became internationally famous when they launched the "Information Awareness Office" a program for the U.S government. It's an abomination of human rights as the government can browse through internet activities, credit card purchases, car rentals, tax returns and any other personal details by the uses of this new government Fakebook called Facebook.

CHAPTER 17

THE REASON FOR RACIST WHITE AMERICANS TO HATE, DEMONIZE, AND LOOK DOWN ON BLACKS

I know that most of you are thinking why talk about a subject that is so sensitive and so racist to say the least. Well because I think it's important, and no matter how much this topic might offend some of you. It's still a part of one of Americans most disturbing evils.

I notice that, plenty of poor whites are racist. About all they have to show for it is this. "At least I'm not black." And that gives it away, it is about white self-image. Now my understanding of this white self-image is that they have no true sense of self-worth, they will put up a false front to sway the world, and most of all themselves that they do have worth. They mainly do this through money, but also by putting down others to make themselves look better, but deep down they know the whole thing is a lie, which makes them all the more desperate to uphold the front. Their racist films often have characters who are either all good or all evil. When they are ask about it they say that of course they know the world is not that simple, that it is just a storytelling device. Yet much of their thinking is very either/or, black or white. The movie

Planet of The Apes or the film King Kong are good examples, not the new remakes but the old ones. In which it reveals a revelation to every racist white American that has a sense of common awareness, that if we don't meaning (whites) kill all the blacks/apes they are going to take over. If you remember in the old Planet of the Apes movie, that there were no blacks being enslaved by the apes only whites. There's another thing I like to point out about the movie. Is that you had three types of primate groups, one was the chimpanzee who represented the many brown skin blacks in the world, who are more radical in nature. That's why Caesar was a chimpanzee, he was brown in the face. Next, you had the orangutan who we will call the light skin brother who was the wiser one of them all because he was whiter than the rest, they control the government. And last and not lease you had the ape, the blackest one of them all in the face. They played the role as tough, aggressive, and most of all dumb.

Now there is another movie I like to point out, and that is King Kong. Now the story has it that King Kong represented the King of Congo, when Christian missionaries came to the country, the King became infatuated with a white female that cause the fall of his empire. Now let's think about it, why in the world would a gigantic ape go all the way to New York, grab this white girl and with all the tall buildings insight to choose from, picks the empire state building to climb and fall from. Do you now get it? This black man/ape man fell from his empire because of a blonde hair, blue eye, white woman.

Now I have never understood why hate groups, such like the Aryan Brotherhood would refer to blacks as monkeys or apes, but a deeper look into this racist insult made me to conclude that it's their way of hiding their own shameful identity. And the reason why I say this is because (1). Blacks don't have thin lips like monkeys or apes. (2).Blacks have kinky woolly hair, and it's not straight like a monkey or ape. Most black people don't grown hair all over their bodies as do monkeys either. (3). If you shave a monkey its skin color would be whitish, far different from brown or black. (4). Monkeys have tails, and if you do some research you will find out that there are people who are born with tails. Now the big shocker is that none of these findings were connected to the so-called black race, but was find to be related to the Caucasian and Mongol races. So this is what it mean about the pot calling the kettle black.

You got to understand that every single black person in the eyes of these racist dogs is a sign of what they wish they were, a reminder that their life is a fraud, that they are pretty much nothing more than armed robbers. It's hard for them to simply own up to their past and make it right. Instead they deny, shift blame, lie, twist facts and make black folks into these creatures that they look down on, laugh at and yet, oddly fear. It is a failed attempt to be at peace with themselves and everyone.

CHAPTER 18

IS THERE REALLY A SUCH THING AS THE ILLUMINATI

Now we first need to understand what the illuminati was. Many people think it was, and is some super powered group of individuals bent on world domination. You have to understand that this is a belief concocted by the early church. It has no validity what so ever. Originally they were a group of scientists and intellectuals who opposed the dogmatic teaching found within religion, especially Christianity. Their sole purpose was the advancement of truth. While the Catholic Church was teaching science was of the devil, they were teaching science was of God. They believed science and religion could go hand and hand. If we look at Christianity during its height of power we will see why such a group was necessary. At this time the Catholic Church was imprisoning individuals who made scientific claims that appeared to conflict with the Bible. One prominent example was Galileo who claimed the earth rotated around the sun. For reasons such as this an underground group was necessary simply for their own survival.

Today Christianity no longer has a stranglehold over the world. Individuals can claim whatever they choose without worrying about repercussion from the Church. For this reason the Illuminati is no longer necessary. So no, I'm a 100% sure that the Illuminati is long deceased but have branched off in other such secret groups like the Skulls and Bones, and Masons who are setting of shop all around the world.

CHAPTER 19

THE COMING OF A CASHLESS AMERICA

The technology for a cashless society is marching right towards a world government. We often hear about this "New World Order" and the global elite who are preparing the world for a new international financial and political system, a society controlled by networked computers containing a database of information on everyone.

This shift to electronic commerce has been slow, but people like the swiftness and convenience of electronic exchange, and are now use to it. For years people has operated on paper bills and coins that are real, which gives people a sense of owning something. In that respect, the world hasn't changed that much since coins were first minted. Many people are still uneasy with the idea of a computerized card or chip linking them to their invisible wealth. So the elite must speed up the process towards a cashless economy by showing to the world how much it is needed.

And to do that, the government will continue to use crisis after crisis in the name of whatever, such as identity theft or the war on drugs. One will be an international economic crash, the recession of all time. They will use this recession to overcome the apathy of the status quo. Without such radical intervention, people will change their ways slowly to suit their purposes and fit their time frame.

There will be other reasons and developments that will also make this new economic system seem necessary. Governments will see it as a means of fighting against crime and shorting government spending. Corporation will embrace it as a means of instant payment and automated inventory and accounting, cutting their expenses and thereby increasing their profit. And the people will embrace it for its convenience, security, and ease.

They will also use wars, and fear such like terrorism and epidemics of new incurable diseases. All this stuff will make people scream for change. They will eventually be ready to except anything that the government may throw at them. They will introduce a new monetary system, whereby they will profess that they are fixing the world's economic woes. Those of you who are not aware of this will be trick in accepting a computerized ID card bearing all your personal, financial, and medical information. Big Government will thereby be able to monitor everyone's every move. In fact, there's people who have already accepted these cards, and some have also agreed to receive computer chip implants underneath their skin. These chips are about the size of the tip of a ballpoint pen and can be read by a handheld scanner. When will this become the norm and widely used by corporation and business such as shopping centers and banks? In the next 10 to 15 years because a global cashless economy and a totally monitored and controlled society are in the works. Fiber optics, satellites, and computer databases have the potential to control the world in a way that will boggle the mind.

Many governments and private business everywhere are already pursuing plans to abolish cash and checks, while many other countries are trying out numerous of methods of doing business without physical currency. So we might be seeing a completely cashless society in the immediate future, the foundation has been laid, and the available evidence indicates that we are indeed moving in that direction pretty soon.

CHAPTER 20

YOUR KIDS ARE BEING KIDNAPPED FOR GOVERNMENTPEDOPHILE RINGS

Have you ever wonder why that thousands of children a year are being reported missing and are never found, crazy right? It's true that there are individuals who are pedophiles that kidnap kids, but 90% of the time these sickos usually are caught and is prosecuted by the law, but what is so strange about the whole thing is that a person can get 10 years for stealing a loaf bread and a pedophile only gets six months behind bars or maybe less for molesting someone's innocent child. So why is this? Why is the law so soft on these animals? And that's why most of the thousands of children are never found.

Well right now there is a silent epidemic where children are being legally abducted by social service (CPS) from parents. Although there are some bad parents, there are thousands of really good parents who are living in agony because there children were snatched from them. The secret family courts took away their rights and warned them that if they went public, they would face prosecution. These children often end up being sold for profit or end up in government pedophile rings. Let me elaborate on this before you say what is this guy talking about. A couple of decades ago President Bill Clinton changed the law regarding the (CPS). The (CPS) were told that they had to reach certain targets, and the more children they obtained, the more bonuses they would get. This has led to thousands of kids being wrongfully abducted from caring parents. So the truth is this, the people who control the governments are heavily involved in Satanism and pedophilia activities which goes all way back to ancient Greece's. Their families' bloodlines have a history of molesting and sacrificing kids, and these nasty sickos are worth billions. These people invest lots of money into the (CPS) because it allows them access to children. Many of these kids go missing and end up in these government pedophile rings, all controlled by secret societies.

Why else do you think Jimmy Saville was so close to the Royal Family, and got away with his child molesting for so long?

Human rights and freedom of speech are rapidly diminishing. There have been cases where parents, whose child had cancer, refused poisonous chemotherapy and chose to use natural cures which the government has kept secret all these years. If you want to learn more about cancer cures that have been hidden from us, look up a doctor by the name of Dr. Leonard Coldwell. These parents had their kids taken away and forced to take chemotherapy, and many of them died afterwards. It's coming to the point where parents cannot decide how to treat their own children. If they don't follow the system their kid can get taken away.

Then there is the big vaccination hoax. There are more and more doctors speaking out against the dangers of vaccines and how it's all a big hoax for population control, because these vaccines can cause cancer and many other chronic illnesses. More and more pregnant women and children are being encouraged to get vaccinated. The time will come when it will become law, where kids will have to be vaccine whenever they are told, and parents who refuse will have their children taken away. It's already happened with chemotherapy. Vaccine will be next.

CHAPTER 21

THE GOVERNMENT DRUG CONNECTION

I think that the government is the biggest drug dealer's in America, so this war on drugs mess is just a big cover up. It all started under the Nixon Administration and their attack on marijuana, but Reagan is known as the "Just Say No" President for his campaign against recreational drugs in America and a strong policy of international drug extermination. Now at the time of the Reagan era, Americans were being presented with tough anti – drug propaganda, the CIA was in fact an accomplice to a large narcotics smuggling ring in the United States. It was in fact Reagan's policies that led to the cooperation between the CIA and the Contras. The Contras were a counter revolutionary group that was fighting against the Sandinistas to return the corrupt Somoza regime to power in Nicaragua. In 1986 Reagan made a statement saying: *"Despite our best efforts, illegal cocaine is coming into our country at alarming levels and 4 to 5 million people regularly use it.*"

Reagan knew very well how these illegal drugs was getting into America, and wasn't going to make any effort to stop it either. By 1998 the CIA finally admitted to its involvement in drug trafficking in the United States after years of federal investigation by the Kerry Congressional Committee. What the CIA admitted to was allowing cocaine trafficking to take place by Contras who were being supported by the CIA, using facilities and resources supplied by the US government, and preventing investigation into these activities by other agencies. This was done because funds for the support of militant groups in South America had been withdrawn by Congress so the CIA allowed the Contras to engage in the drug trade in the United States in order to make money to fund their military operations.

If you are wondering why this was not covered more widely in the news during the Clinton Administration, it was because Arkansas was one of the major trafficking centers for the operations.

So the truth is that the "War on Drugs" is more about international politics and control than it is about concern for the health of people. Drugs have been a major factor in the funding of revolutions for centuries. This is because drugs are a very high profit product that can be grown by even the most primitive people, and thus it's very hard to control. In fact the American Revolution was funded by drugs and that drug was tobacco and opium. Hell, tobacco was regulated by the King of England not only for health reason, but also because he knew that it was funding the American colonials.

Also America was able to pay for French support in the war against England largely through tobacco money. At the time the American Revolution was also known as "The Tobacco Wars" and the area of Massachusetts Bay was known as "The Tobacco Coast"

Likewise opium and cocaine have also been products that have funded many wars and revolutions over the few hundred years. In fact, a common strategy for individuals that wish to quickly gain large amounts of money is to sell drugs to their local population which is well predominate in the black community today.

The reason why the Reagan administration began the war on drugs was to cut off the money supply to revolutionary groups in South America, the Middle East, and Asia that were using drug money to fund wars for national independence from foreign intervention. America has been able to selectively apply pressure to various regimes under the guise of the so-called "War on Drugs," which is just one more way that elements of the American government have been able to get funding for taking action against foreign governments in order to promote American interest. Another of the major problems that prompted the origin of the "War on Drugs" and was able to get much of the initial support for the program was the Medellin Cartel in Columbia run by Pablo Escobar. This was a very legitimate and problematic issue; the Medellin Cartel was out of control and terrorizing the country of Columbia. This is really what has always been behind the "War on Drugs," the problem that is being addressed is not drug use, but the existence of drug cartels, terrorism, and political groups that use drugs money to fund private wars. To add on to this, in 1999

129

Congress released a report on the history of the CIA involvement in drug trafficking. A book was written on this called The Politics of Heroin, CIA Complicity in the Global Drug Trade by Alfred McCoy which details first-hand the mechanics of drug trafficking in Asia, Europe, and South and Central America. And about the U.S. involvement in the narcotics trade in Afghanistan and Pakistan before and after the fall of the Taliban, and how U.S. drug policy in Central America and Colombia has increased the global supply of illicit drugs.

CHAPTER 22

THE HOMO-PHOMO AGENDA

Here we are in the year 2016, and with same sex marriage bills, the don't ask, don't tell' policy and same sex couples being able to adopt a child, many feel this lifestyle is being promoted and not just supported. Many people are starting to question if the powers that be have created a "gay agenda" with cruel intentions.

Now up until 1973, homosexuality was listed as a mental disorder in the Diagnostic and Statistical Manual of Mental Disorder. Some say homosexuality is used as a population control strategy which started in 1973 under the Rockefeller World Population Council. The Planned Parent Hood International and the Rockefeller World Population Council decided it would be best that homosexuality be propagated in America society as a healthy lifestyle choice. Also in 1974 a man by the name Dr. Henry Kissinger created a national security memorandum called NSSM2000, a document that looks specifically at strategies to control the population rate across the world such like birth control, healthy sexual practices and an alternative lifestyle modifications. Asia and America along with Africa are listed as targets.

Have you ever wonder why a lot of male celebrities are dressing up in women cloths in movies, it seems that all of them have played either a women or a gay man at least once in their careers. Couldn't the director find a woman to play the role? Why are these men being asked to put on dresses?

Dave Chappelle is a comedian and actor who walked away from a $50 million dollar contract because he didn't agree with what was taken place behind the scenes in Hollywood. In 2006, during an interview with Oprah, Chappelle talks about how he was asked to wear a dress multiple times on the set of the film, "Blue Streak." He says many different people (writers, directors, and producers) tried to convince him to wear it. He says they finally backed off after he continuously said no. Chappelle told Oprah he wondered why he'd seen so many men in dresses in film and television. He also said, *"You have to take a stand."*

Now also women are being masculinized which resulted in lesbianism, many of them have been molested, mistreated or have witnessed domestic violence by a man they loved or trusted. I don't think that all women turn gay because of this reason, I do believe it's a chemical imbalance in the brain, very much like when someone is born with two sexual parts or extra limbs. I hate when people say only God is perfect, if that was true then his creation should be perfect. Because you can't be perfect and create imperfection. So see a lot of this gay mess is a mental disorder that can't be cured just like you can't cure craziness.

Apart from that, nothing better demonstrates society than the elite's attempt to make everyone behave like homosexuals, and up until 1973 gays was recognized for what it is, (a developmental disorder). Then, overnight it was redefined as a "lifestyle choice," one that government, schools and media actively promoted.

In the military, soldiers now have to live in close quarters with openly gay men. This is like putting sex crazed men in a room with gorgeous young women. No it won't affect military capability. And as they are doing now universalizing "gay marriage."

Thanks to feminism, which is many ways is lesbian, the day is fast approaching when people will lose interest in the opposite sex. They will decide that the other sex has nothing to offer in terms of love, marriage and family. The new family model will be single-parents or homosexuals raising the products of one night stands and sperm clinics. The government goal is to redefine and manipulate human beings by taken away the family identity. For example the movie "Brokeback Mountain" was part of this revolutionary crusade to mainstream homosexuality. Throughout history these devils of society have used every tactic in the bag to trick people into behaving self destructively. Effective propaganda mixes truth with deception.

In Brokeback Mountain it's telling people that gay love often has tragic consequences. At the end of the movie, Ennis is a pathetic figure living alone in a run-down trailer. He treasures items of clothing that once belonged to his lover Jack, who died in a gay beat down hit.

Now you see, the deception lies in the movie's assumption that it is normal and natural for men to engage in homosexual behavior. These men do not look or act gay and as cowboys, they engage in masculine activities. The actors aren't gay. So they will say. "I'm not a faggot," the other says. "Me neither," Then they jump into the bed together. So the implication here is that all men are in denial.

In the real world men and women naturally find homosexual sex distasteful, a fact the movie tacitly recognizes by mercifully portraying little of it. The movie image of homosexuality is sanitized and made to seem just like heterosexuality. In fact, a faithful long term relationship like this one is exceptional.

For example, in Holland male homosexual relationships last on average, 1.5 years, and a gay man have an average of eight partners a year outside of their supposedly "committed" relationships. No matter how much the media disguise it, most gays won't sex not marriage.

Now back to this movie Brokeback Mountain, so these two cowboys aren't typical homosexuals and they certainly aren't normal heterosexuals. In the movie they mention they were alienated from their biological fathers at a young age.

Ennis' parents died in a car accident while Jack's father rejected him. It seems that these Homosexual males are trying to compensate for their loss. Another cause maybe sexual abuse on the youth. But a lot of these people have been born that way because of a testosterone imbalance during gestation. In spite of the fact that they want you to believe that homosexuality is usually the result of father - loss or sexual abuse, the government is pushing this disability on society.

They are using the tired guilt tactics they use in promoting their other "oppressed minorities" for socially subversive ends.

They accuse people like me of bigotry, but so what! Homosexual rights, disguises a malicious undercover attack on heterosexuals because we don't submit to it.

This society militates against healthy marriage and families. Men are no longer being taught that manhood involves supporting and raising a family.

So you see heterosexuality is much more than opposite sex attraction. It's about monogamy (marriage) reproduction and child rearing. This is how most of us develop and fulfill ourselves. Obviously, these natural process is also essential for societal health. This society militates against healthy marriage and families. Men no longer learn that being a man is about supporting and raising a family. Women waste their most fertile years at a college, learning to fear and compete with men. The media encourages them to be hoes, and experiment with lesbianism. May I go on?

To me homosexuality is a part of a developmental disorder resulting in failure to permanently bond with a member of the opposite sex. This has become a common social illness as divorce rates soar and marriage and birth rates plummet.

Generally speaking, homosexuality is characterized by a belief in sex for its own sake and an obsession on sex appeal as the main principle of personal worth. Haven't we all submitted in many ways?

People don't understand that these politicians' leaders are selling us out in the dirtiest fashion. They have literally sold out to the government elite, a secret society that promote pedophilia, human sacrifice, and every form of degradation, corruption and organized crime. They stage wars and atrocities, like the September 11 massacre for-profit and power. They are right now secretly plotting a one world police state.

It's not so much a secret anymore as it was in the past, the internet has made it hard for them to hide their devious plan. So I'm not here just to talk down on gays because at the end of the day these people can do whatever they want to do, it doesn't make a damn to me. My argument is with the (Rockefeller Foundation) social engineers who markets homosexuality as a weapon to strip the social fabric and enslave us. We are not going to be fooled by their insults and hypocritical appeals to "tolerance." We will defend ourselves.

CHAPTER 23

THE UNSEEN HAND

In these next few subjects I like to speak about the secretive agenda of the power elite and events that will take place in the near future. I will present as much info as I can, exposing these wealthily groups and families and their secretive agenda.

A lot of you may say, that this is just another conspiracy theory and it's nothing more than bullsh*t, but I will do my best to present credible facts and I also encourage the reader to do their own research.

President George H.W. Bush announcement on 16 January 1991 of allied military action in the Persian Gulf:

"We in this past year made great progress in ending the long era of conflict, and cold war. We have before us the opportunity to forge for ourselves and for future generations have a "New World Order," a world where the rule of law, not the law of the jungle, governs the conduct of nations. When we are successful,

and we will be. We have a real chance at this "New World Order,"
an order in which a credible United Nations can use its
peacekeeping role to fulfill the promise and vision of the U.N.'s
founders...."

That quotation above and many others like them, clearly demonstrates that the words "New World Order" is for real, and have been in use for decades. It did not originate with President George Bush in 1990. The "Old World Order" is based on independent nation-states. The "New World Order" involves the elimination of the sovereignty and the independence of nation-states and turn it into some form of world government. This means the end of the United States, the U.S. Constitution, and the Bill of Rights as we now know them. The plan is to involve the conversion of the United Nations and its agencies to a world government, complete with a world army, a world parliament, a world court, global taxation, and numerous of other agencies to control every aspect of your life. Such as education, nutrition, health care, population, immigration, communication, transportation, commerce, agriculture, finance, the environment, etc. The various notions of this order differ as to details and scale, but has the same basic principle and substance.

You must understand, in order to take control over a people, and governor them utterly is to take a little of their freedom at a time, for example. (The Patriot Act) that was passed just 45 days after 9/11. The NDAA Act, Affordable Healthcare Act, The expansion of drone program, The NSA domestic spying program, the Real ID Act, private prisons. They are doing this in the UK too, with militarized police, police drones, NGI databases, signing waivers to the "Armed Control Export Act" to circumvent the constitution. In this way the people will not see their rights being removed until pass the point at which these changes cannot be reversed.

WHO'S REALLY THE POWER PLAYERS?

The power players are made up largely of wealthy bankers who controls the mainstream media, workforce, education system, companies, local banks, energy supplies and governments. These super-rich families are the Rothschild and the Rockefeller. They also the driving force behind organizations such as the United

Nations, the WTO and the Council on Foreign Relations. Their main plan is to control the world's money, which would mean full control over everyone, especially those in debt. This is exactly what these families are doing, every government is in debt to them. This debt is increasing, especially personal debt because of wasteful spending, borrowing is encouraged. Therefore people and governments are becoming increasingly in the control of the international bankers by having to pay interest, which the bankers can manipulate to their will.

Governments are forced to sell assets, lose sovereignty, and place citizens in poverty to repay their debt. These people are privatizing, buying and controlling government assets. They also bribe governments with political donations. They gain ownership of land through world heritage, which is mismanaged and restricted.

To prove there's a plan for world control, just look at the rising amount of globalization, free trade, privatization, foreign investment, mergers, international organization, debt, international problems that need an international solution, and peace agreements that give false security.

Perhaps the greatest trick is to distract you from the truth, so that you will lose money and property to the powerful elite, who corruptly monopolize wealth and power as a result. Instead of using your time and money to fight. You are deceived into spending more money than you really have, so that you will lose it to the powerful elite. A common control measure is to convince the majority that the purpose of life is to eat, drink and be merry.

WHO'S IDEA OF WORLD DOMINATION?

The foundation for modern day secret domination was laid by a man name Cecil Rhodes, a British imperialist in South Africa, who advocated a one world government controlled by Anglo-Saxons. His view was that, the British Empire had the right to rule Africa, parts of Asia and all of North America, include Canada, Australia and New Zealand.

Rhodes was a Freemason and established a Rhodesian secret society to further his goal for Anglo-Saxon rule. This secret society created the Roundtable group and ultimately the (Council on Foreign Relations) which is known to be the architect of most of the policies of the US government. Majority of CFR members also into masonry.

The powerful elites at the helm of these groups desire nothing short of total control of the people. There is a global cartel of financial institutions that is able to dominate the political system of each country and its economy, thereby influencing governments and their policies.

To implement their agenda in the U.S. this group used their influence in the government and the congress to establish the Federal Reserve System, a banking establishment which was controlled by this cartel of private banks. The Federal Reserve was then allowed to print money and loan it to the government on interest.

THE FEDERAL RESERVE AND ITS CONTROL OF THE WORLD ECONOMY:

So what does the Federal Reserve have to do with world control? Well to really understand the whole story, you need to understand how the bankers work. Here's what one of the so-called founding fathers said, Thomas Jefferson.

"I believe that banking institutions are more dangerous to our liberties than standing armies. If the American people ever allow private banks to control the issues of their currency, first by inflation, then by deflation, the banks and corporations that will grow up around {the banks} will deprive the people of all property until their children wake-up homeless on the continent their fathers conquered. The issuing power should be taken from the banks and restored to the people, to whom it properly belongs."

This is exactly what's going on today. The dollar is at its lowest spending point in over 60 years. Approximately 1% of the population, around 3 million people, are homeless. Inflation and gas prices are out of control and people are losing their savings. It seems very likely that the younger generation will be worse off than their parents, with the international bankers as the stock owners, the Federal Reserve will continue to be manipulated to protect the banks.

THE PLAN TO DEPOPULATE THE WORLD

One of the main goals of the global elite is to control the population of the world. Their plan is to bring down the population to 2000 million. This goal of depopulation is already in progress and being executed through several programs.

One of these programs are called the "Codex Alimentarius," which is administered by the United Nations and is a published nutritional guideline. The health agencies of different countries are under these guidelines to determine what you can or cannot consume. And the consumptions of vitamins and minerals is discouraged by attempting to classify them as drugs.

The global food supply is also manipulated by genetically modifying the crops and changing their nutritional characteristics. This genetic modification is extremely dangerous and can cause preventable diseases resulting in millions of deaths.

Another weapon used against the masses is the fluoridation of water supplies. In most cities, the water coming into people homes contains fluoride which is added in by the city corporations. Fluoride is an industrial toxin and is poisonous. It was used by the Nazis to control aggressive behavior in the people in their concentration camps. Case in point, is a compound used in many anti-depressants like Prozac.

Fluoride is also known to be the cause for a number of medical problems, including cancer, bone disease, immune deficiency, mental sedation, and it can even cause a reduced IQ.

Vaccines are given to people especially young children that contain traces of mercury. People are lining up for flu shots without realizing that they are being poisoned.

Also the government has been spreading toxins in the air by using airplanes. Other techniques used in their quest is nuclear warfare, starvation, and biological attacks like the bird flu.

NO ONE IS FREE, YOU ARE THE PROPERTY OF THE STATE

If the government can tell you what you can and cannot do within the privacy of your home, whether it relates to what you eat, what you smoke or whom you go out with, you no longer have any rights whatsoever within your home.

If government officials can fine and arrest you for growing vegetables in your front yard, play cards with friends in your living room, installing solar panels on your roof, and raising sheep's in your backyard, you're no longer the owner of your property. If school officials can interfere in your child's family affairs for what they do or say while at home or in your care, your children are not your own, they are the property of the state.

If government agents can invade your home, break down your doors, kill your dog, damage your furniture and terrorize your family, your property is no longer private and secure, it belongs to the government. Likewise, if police can forcefully draw your blood, strip search you, and analysis you intimately, your body is no longer your own either. LIKE I SAID YOU ARE THE PROPERTY OF THE STATE!

WHAT TO EXPECT IN THE NEXT DECADE

In the next decade or so there will be plans to create a whole different government, one that will force the current government to suspend the Constitution and confiscate all guns in American homes.

By doing this they will first create civil unrest in all major US cities, like New York, Chicago, Atlanta, etc. This will be preceded by months of subconscious programming through TV, radio and other media outlets to condition the people for civil war in the United States. Special agents of the conspiracy will masquerade as policemen, and will open fire on the people standing to defend their Constitution rights. Next, the protesters will eventually become violent and will fire back on the real policemen. This brings in more police, and the peaceful protests turns out to become a complete riot.

Inner city gangs already fully armed, joins in the fight. The police is now vastly outnumbered, and cannot handle the rioting. The National Guard is called in and fired upon by other special agents masquerading as gang members, who also enlists other gang members to fight the police and the National Guard.

If this scenario fails to materialize into a national state of emergency, they may attempt an all-out United Nations invasion of the US, using whatever possible means they can to justify such a UN operation.

Next, they will plan a crash of the stock market which will dramatic drop to a lease 1700 on the DJ industrial average. Along with the death of the US dollar. This event is planned to further weaken, and put panic, and confuse the population. Followed by a failure in the US food chain delivery system, meaning food shortage will become a problem. There will be mass unemployment, mortgage defaults, huge individual and national debts. The people will be begging for answers and real leadership, the problem will become global to make the people believe that a global solution is necessary.

The people would then be introduced to a microchip implants, in order to control this so-called war on terror.

There will also be new viruses to begin reducing the population, providing mandatory vaccinations in order to get people to believe that it's a cure, but it will not save lives but only speed up the process.

There will be more fake terror attacks to give encouragement to the people to voluntarily give up the remainder of their personal rights.

There will be also attacks on countries that are not in line with the global elite, such countries like Iran, North Korea Russia, and one that you might not believe, "Yes, Saudi Arabia.

Of course these are some of my predictions of the future, but there is also a few I like to share with the brothers and sisters that are incarcerated across this nation. That in the next 5 years or so the US government will be bringing back the draft, which will mean that newly released inmates who has nonviolent felonies will be automatically forced into the military. This is the reason why they are allowing people with felonies to vote, when in the past that was a no-no.

There will be states around the nation that will be nearly bankrupt, and will begin charging inmates for their three hot's and a cot the moment they are released. They will be given the restitution fee order from the court, and the amount they owe while they were incarcerated.

They will also end all physical face-to-face visits, which means visitation will be conducted on screen monitors so that all drugs and contraband won't get inside the prisons. Also weightlifting will no longer be allowed, prisoners with long sentences will be sent to do their time in other countries due to overcrowding, and 95% of the food will be artificial, and what they called the nutritional loaf will be your everyday main course. Also inmates will be forced to shave the hair off their head and face, and they will no longer be allow to purchase personal books or magazines of any sort. These changes will occur as policies in the so-called free world begins to develop closer and closer to a global police state.

CHATPER 24

THE FINAL CONCLUSION

The question I'm most often asked is "If what you're saying is true, then what is the solution, what do I do to protect myself and my family?" Well the answer to that question is not all that easy, trust me. Because if it was, it wouldn't be no need for the publication of this book. But don't make no mistake about it, there is a lot we can do, we don't have to be waiting around for them to put shackles on us.

Our number one weapon when dealing with an enemy is your knowledge, because with that knowledge, and after years of learning to think how to live primarily independent of the system. Never rely the beast/government to save you from the trap that he planned for you, because don't forget who's responsible for this mess in the first place!

WHAT IS A RATIONAL PERSON TO DO?

1. Develop a substitute income supply instead of depending on a 9 to 5 job.

2. Make sure that your personal affairs are in order, because you don't want to do anything that can possibly land you in jail.

3. Make sure you're in good physical shape to survive any sort of city outbreak that can possibly happen such as a nationwide uprising or catastrophe.

4. Reduce your television watching to no more than two hours a day and convert to a more productive means of elevate your mind, like reading a book or mediating.

5. Avoid scandalous, traditional mainstream news services, who are intent on keeping you deaf dumb and blind, try to choose mainly independent news services.

6. Be careful what you do on the internet. Otherwise government watchdogs can find out anything you do online.

7. Develop a survivalist mindset in case of a food and water shortages, and for many of the people who depends on government checks every month and food stamps should be preparing for a financial safe haven. Because in the next 20 years or so, the government will shut down for good.

8. Learn how to not worry too much, in the midst of worsening circumstances because whatever the situation might be, it's all going to work out in the end.

BREAKING THE SHACKLES OFF THE MIND

Reducing the exposure of manipulation is actually sort of easy, although it does take effort. Part of it is just becoming conscious of the methods of manipulation by thinking deeply about them, but this must be accompanied by an effort to push against the norm, against what everybody else does, however it's a small price to pay when one considers that democracy itself and the freedom of your children future is at stake. Manipulation may well be a common thing in society, but the following steps will be more than enough to protect us against its influence.

STEP ONE
Stop watching so much television

Turn it off! There is no other distraction that causes more confusion and manipulation than television, with its neuron-numbing soundbites, dissociated facts and images. It's huge vulnerability to government and corporate propaganda, due to almost 100% big business ownership. It's distortion of the most serious situations from war to social disturbance, and its menacing presence in every home. Television has become the number one tool for manipulating society.

STEP TWO

Don't consume yourself into debt

It's easy for some but impossible for many, but even if one could, and sacrifices are needed to do so. It is better not to be in debt, as the contract of a debt such as mortgage, borrowing money etc. manipulates you into being a slave. When many unfortunately have no choice, as their very survival has created debt. It is concerning that there are a huge and growing number of people who are in debt not because they can't afford food and shelter, but because they have bought into the propaganda that they need a faster car, bigger house and the latest flat screen television.

STEP THREE
Think outside the box

This is the hardest and the most profound of all the steps to stop manipulation, and it comes from a combination of self-education, and self-focus. A mind that knows itself knows how to be free and knows when it is being manipulated. It is a fact that those who have substantially practiced meditation or conscious introspection has find it far easier to know when another person is lying or trying to manipulate them. Whether meditation means sitting cross-legged in front of an object of your choice or walking out alone in a quiet area practicing freedom of the mind, self-knowledge makes you much more aware of the processes of enslavement.

Well, there are several things you can do right now to make sure that you are mentally, physically and spiritually prepare for the coming hard times. You can call me crazy or whatever but you must plan now and be ready to implement that plan the moment that this shit jumps off. Yes, the vast majority of the world is controlled by a few, and they establish harsh laws through the approval of the ignorant masses. Everything that the wide masses of people approve is likely to be very bad for you.

So what can we do about it? Form some type of group? Pick up guns and sticks and fight the system? Talk about it? Start marching up and down the street? Hell no! Marching is for suckers. And we are not suckers. That's why those awakening to the truth are usually alone. They realize that marching is a waste of time and foolish. And after all, those who do march are program to believe that it is the right thing to do.

The sign that a person is not program is when he/she refuses to belong to any religion, company, or organization. Even worse, organizations tend to become violent or one-sided with time. Organizations become corrupt with time. Organization leaders become power thirsty and greedy. And will not accomplish nothing.

So I would suggest another way. Follow your own truth, do you. You can open people eyes by the way you live. Share your positive energy with others. Show them through your example. Don't try to change no one, simply live the best way you can. For example.

TRY TO GROW YOUR ON FOOD

If possible, grow your own food. If not, buy locally grown food from small business owners. If this is not possible, at least buy fruits and vegetables instead of buying artificial foods.

NEVER FEAR NOTHING

Because fear is the fuel of those power thirsty individuals who wants power over you. So please, never fear. Fear equals weakness, fear equals extremely low energy. Don't even get angry as this is also the negative energy that people can feed on. Fear is neutralized by knowledge and wisdom and raising your vibrations. Don't listen to all that crazy stuff in the media. Pay attention to what's in front of you, and what you can control.

DO YOUR OWN THING AND NEVER FOLLOW ANYONE

Because even following a positive person, is a mistake. They will get you off your own path. You can use them to raise your vibration, but you will have to find your path on your own. That's because each path is unique. Listen to your heart. Stop doing what cause problems and unhappiness in you. For example, if you hate going to work each and every day, it's obvious that you need to find another job to do. It's killing your soul.

EACH ONE SHOULD TEACH ONE

If there are people who are willing to listen to what you have to say, then teach them as much as you can. Those who are ready to hear about what's happening in the world should be enlightened as much as possible. They are ready to be awaken, and they are looking for someone who knows the truth.

DON'T OVERLOAD YOUR MIND WITH BOGUS INFORMATION

Don't believe everything you read or hear on television. You would just end up feeling drained, confused and negative. Instead work on things that only you can improve, listen to your inner self, and raise your vibrations. You will help yourself better this way than focusing on things that you cannot change.

PROTECT YOURSELF MENTALLY

I mean try not to get involved in vibrational lowering situations. Such as never in danger yourself with a fool or talking to energy sucking people.

LIVE YOUR OWN TRUTH

Because your life is so different to the life of another that sometimes you feel that you are not of this world. That's called living your own truth.

For example, some people call me strange. I love it, because I know I'm living my truth. I do everything that feels right to me rather than what other people think is right. I don't own a house, nor do I want to own one. I feel perfectly okay renting a house. I like getting up at night with inspired thoughts to write down. That's why some people call me strange. I am strange, because I live my own truth. I hope you do too peace.

CPSIA information can be obtained at www.ICGtesting.com
Printed in the USA
LVOW11s1534210916

505620LV00001B/153/P